THE HEART
OF SUCCESS

This book redefines the concept of success. It has some answers for people who are succeeding in business but beginning to ask themselves whether there is more to life than they are currently achieving. It could change your life if you dare act on the thoughts it raises for you.

*I challenge leaders in industry to dedicate half an hour in successive management meetings for discussion with their teams of a chapter from **The Heart of Success**. I guarantee it will revolutionise relationships and work effectiveness.*

I would recommend CEOs to give a copy of this book to every manager in their company.

Jim Wright, Vice-President of Human Resources, SmithKline Beecham R&D

Before you read one more book on how to climb the corporate ladder read this: it will help you make sure the ladder is leaning against the right wall.

Kevin Kaiser, Adjunct Professor of Finance, INSEAD, and Vice-President of Product Development, bfinance.com

*Rob has the unique ability to demonstrate how we can get the balance right between the pressures of business and the demands of family life. His seminars and **The Heart of Success** book will help you in the on-going battle to achieve success in both arenas.*

Chris Street, Vice-President and General Manager of Global Customer Services, Alcatel

Rob Parsons is one of the most inspirational speakers in the country today. **The Heart of Success** *has the same ingredients as his presentations – motivating, practical and giving you the sense that somebody has just turned a light on.*

Rosemary Conley, author, broadcaster and Chairman of the Rosemary Conley Group

Rob Parsons has an uncanny ability for asking some of life's most challenging questions in an unobtrusive way. If you need to take time to reflect on who you are, what you value, and how you can live more of the life you believe in, then this book is a great place to start.

Jill Garrett, Managing Director, The Gallup Organisation, UK

This will be the most talked about business book of the year – it is essential reading for anybody who is concerned about genuine people and business development.

Professor Jim Saker, Business School, Loughborough University

Stress, burn-out and absenteeism due to illness are becoming the hallmarks of some companies. That's bad for people and for profits. We need a rapid reversal of this trend and I believe that the principles behind **The Heart of Success** *are absolutely vital to achieve it.*

Dr John Gallacher, psychologist and Senior Research Fellow, University of Wales

*This is an excellent book, full of truth and wisdom.
I would highly recommend it. It contains powerful,
sobering, life-changing lessons that we should spend
time to ponder on.*

**Professor Leslie Lim, President, Singapore Association of
Mental Health**

The Heart of Success *should be on the required
reading list of every university and business school
that seeks to equip its students for life as well as
career. It should be part of the induction course in
every corporation which declares its people to be its
greatest asset.*

**Michael Bates, Director of Consultancy and Research, Oxford
Analytica, and former HM Paymaster-General**

*So many of us crave for significance in our lives and
in our work. This book opens up a way to finding it.*

**John Evans, Senior Economist, Organisation for Economic
Co-operation and Development**

*You can make a meaningful difference in your life,
career, and world, helping those you work with do the
same. This book will catalyse you and your colleagues
– share it wisely and watch the growth.*

**Stephen Horswell, Regional Director, AXA, and former President of
the Life Insurance Association**

*An excellent book for busy people – to reflect, slow
down and modify focus. Try applying a principle a
week and see the change in your life.*

Kang Choon Pin, Partner, Arthur Andersen

A gifted story-teller, unwrapping words of wisdom that demand attention.

Rob W. Garvey, Purchasing Director, University of Bristol

Should be required reading for every executive … There is a new era developing in the business world that embodies working smarter not harder to achieve success.

David Hanks, Executive Vice-President, Riviana Foods Inc.

Our commitment is to give this book to every client we work with – it's that important.

John Tucker and Ian Williams, co-founders of Kairos Business & Family Consulting

It is a book that provides practical advice to today's busy executives. It is an invaluable tool that helps balance family and career demands and, at the same time, moulds character traits that will lay a solid foundation for a life worth living.

James Chia, President, Pico Art International Pte Ltd

The message is crystal clear and positive … the 'hardnosed' business person will benefit most.

Jorgen Oest-Larsen, former Director, Carlsberg International, and Vice-President International, Riviana Foods Inc.

This book is too important to be read only once.

**Patrick Parkinson, Professor of Law and Pro-Dean,
University of Sydney**

*Not just a business book for senior managers, **The
Heart of Success** tells you how to survive in the
working world and achieve a healthy balance
between life and work.*

Jimmy Campbell, postal worker

THE HEART
OF SUCCESS

MAKING IT IN BUSINESS
WITHOUT LOSING IN LIFE

ROB PARSONS

Hodder & Stoughton

British Library Cataloguing in Publication Data
A record for this book is available from the British Library

ISBN 0 340 78623 X

Printed and bound in Great Britain by Bookmarque Ltd, Croydon

Hodder & Stoughton
A Division of Hodder Headline Ltd
338 Euston Road
London NW1 3BH

This book is dedicated to:

- the staff at Merlyn Rees Community High School, Leeds, who are doing an incredible job in a school with such challenging circumstances;

- the children at that school who have so much ability and so many dreams;

- and to all those in the business world who are prepared to become, for some child somewhere ... a dream-catcher.

CONTENTS

Acknowledgments

People often say that books are a joint effort; this one really is. Jonathan Mason has worked with me from the beginning.

Special thanks also to Jonathan Barber, Samantha Callan, Jill Garrett, Bruce Gordon, Robert Gorzynski, Kate Hancock, Ron Lockwood, Dave Phillips, Mike Rimmington and Steve Williams. The team at Hodder Headline, especially Judith Longman, Charles Nettleton and Julie Hatherall, have been brilliant – no author could ask for more.

My good friend, Owain Williams, never fails to encourage me.

Grateful thanks to John Loosemoore, who was my business partner for over twenty-five years.

And, of course, to Jonathan Booth and Sheron Rice, thank you.

I have been speaking on the principles behind *The Heart of Success* for over twenty years in seminars across the world. During those times I have introduced countless people about to embark upon a business career, as well as the companies that employed them, to Professor Murray's seven laws of business and life. This book allows me to give my perspective on each of those laws. But before we begin I want you to meet the professor himself and the young MBA student whose life was changed forever by a chance meeting in a musty library. For this you must come back with me over a quarter of a century ...

MEET THE
PROFESSOR

The Professor and the MBA

Some said that Professor Tom Murray had been around the business school almost as long as the foundations. Certainly not a living soul could recall a time when he wasn't there and nobody really knew how old he was – except that he was very old. He had always worn his hair long, a fact that had robbed some of his 1960s classes of a sense of rebellion, and he still had every strand of it; but now it was snow-white and gave him the look of an Old Testament prophet.

He was an unusual professor. First, he had never written a book. Every publisher in the country had beaten a path to Tom's door but he would always give the same answer, 'I love to teach. If I was writing, I wouldn't be teaching and I'd miss it.' But Tom Murray had never been just an academic. Right behind the publishers had been the CEOs of many of the Fortune 500 companies all wanting 'a little help with a small problem we have'. To these, Tom always said yes. He loved to get involved with companies and, more importantly, with the people who worked in them. And so he had stories: stories that would take a dry business theory, shake the dust from it, and make it live; stories of companies that were 'unsinkable' but had gone down faster than the fated liner; and stories of 'no hope' ideas that had not just broken into markets, but created them.

And Professor Murray was loved by his students. They loved his teaching and they loved his stories. But more than his teaching, and even more than his stories, his students loved him. *It sounds improbable, even a little too emotional, but it was true. He still got letters from men and women who had sat in his freshman class and were now heading huge corporations. Very often they just told him about their lives – their kids, their marriages or the break-up of them, their hopes and their fears. He had been a surrogate father to more of his students than he cared to remember.*

Tom was unusual for just one more reason. His best friend for over fifty years had been Clarke Lewis, the college janitor. Clarke was even older than Tom, but they had played bridge together once a week for as long as they could remember and almost every evening since Tom had retired ten years ago. Except on a Monday. On a Monday Clarke went to visit his daughter and her family fifteen miles away and on that evening Tom locked up the library for him. Of course it was kind of the professor to help his friend out, but in truth he enjoyed doing it: it gave him an excuse to walk the aisles again; to handle the books; to savour the musty scent of the old building.

He had loved the library from the day he first walked through its huge wooden doors. It stood atop the hill overlooking the university campus. Its Victorian architecture looked down in more ways than one on the trendy glass buildings that made up the remainder of academia in the great city. No fluorescent lighting in this shrine of business studies: glistening chandeliers hung from the high ornate ceilings. They cast uneven light, not really suited to reading the small print but, in a building that held tomes on efficiency, this gesture to the greatness of another age seemed to exist without criticism.

Not only did books line the walls but also the floors, the alcoves and the walnut desks that students leant on, dozed on and, on one occasion, drew on. The dean of studies *never did discover the identity of the tormented soul who had carved, 'The living are the dead on holiday', and it seemed sufficiently philosophical to have escaped the French-polisher's hand.*

And what books they were! Books that stretched back over 300 years of economics and management theory. Books that had topped bestseller lists and then fallen from grace; books that in their time had been provocative and were now boringly acceptable; books that promised success; and books that carefully catalogued failure.

Every evening at 9.45 exactly, the janitor sounded the bell that shattered the hallowed silence of the main library to warn the readers, wake the sleepers and announce the pending closure of the building at 10 p.m. sharp. But as the professor shuffled along the aisles on the night of Monday 8 October he knew there was hardly any need to sound the bell: row upon row of empty desks stretched in front of him; the great hall was deserted.

But Clarke had given him strict instructions on the way things were always done, and so Tom dutifully lifted the bronze gavel and struck the huge gong. Even sound, it seemed, moved around the great hall with respect and slowness. The deep notes of the bell resonated through the library. They crawled past Adam Smith's Wealth of Nations, *slithered into the recesses where dwelt* Any Colour Just So Long as It's Black: A Short History of the Ford Motor Company *and skirmished along the aisles of the more modern offerings. Past book upon book, theory upon theory, team building and individualism, quality circles and bottom lines, booms and busts, recessions and revivals, depressions and deliverance, bears and bulls, IQ, EQ and dole queue.*

And then Tom saw it: a shadow moving at the far end, just past 'Industrial Periodicals' and the Harvard Business Review *shelves. He blinked twice; his eyes weren't as good as they had been. Whether he was shocked, scared or just annoyed he couldn't tell, but whatever emotion he felt caused him to do something that in all his years of walking the aisles of the great hall he had never done before: Tom raised his voice. 'Is anybody there?'*

The young man who stepped out of the aisle and into the pale light looked more scared than Tom. He made his way towards the professor.

'Don't you have a home to go to, son?'

'I'm sorry, sir. I got kind of engrossed. I'll leave straight away.'

'No, you're fine – the library has another fifteen minutes.'

'No – I guess I'm finished.'

'Can I help you in any way?'

If the young man had any idea to whom he was speaking he would have left straight away, but the old janitor seemed harmless and he was anxious to talk.

'Sir, tomorrow I begin my MBA. My father died last year. He was a CEO and his great ambition was for me to study here and carve a career in business that would make him proud. My dad was successful in almost everything he did. He built a company from nothing into a multimillion-pound operation; he broke into markets that others thought impossible. The Harvard Business Review *called him, "A success story without parallel".'*

'Well, son, I'm sure if he could see you now he would be proud. Try to follow his example.' Tom turned to leave but the young man caught his arm.

'I said my father was successful in almost everything he did. It's that "almost" that has brought me to the library today. I didn't see much of him when I was a boy. When other parents watched their kids in football matches my dad could never make it. Once when I had the lead in a school play he turned up just as the curtain was falling. We had a home with twenty rooms and a private jet. I had toys the others kids could only dream of. The only thing I didn't have was him.

'My dad had fifteen thousand employees, twelve board members and no real friends. He'd been to a thousand business lunches but in the end there was nobody he felt he could really talk to about himself. When we had a party for his sixtieth birthday, five hundred people came. At his funeral there were fifty. My dad died too young. He just pushed himself too hard. I'm not sure I want the success he had at the price he paid. And I have scoured these titles today for the answer to one simple question: "What does it mean to be successful – can you make it and still have a life?"'

Tom had five children, ten grandchildren, and hundreds of former students he still thought of as family. He had seen the look on this boy's face a thousand times. This *young man was desperate. He motioned for the student to pull up one of the empty chairs.*

'Son, I have a confession for you. I'm not the janitor. I'm retired now, but I have taught business studies at this great institution for longer than I care to remember.'

The young student's eyes were wide and he pulled his chair in closer as Tom went on. 'More than that, I have followed the careers and business endeavours of the men and women who have written the books on success. I can tell you that some of them made more money out of their books than they ever made out of their companies. But even then the success they seemed to enjoy was a one-dimensional thing. Some of these people didn't have time to spit, let alone watch a sunset; some of them had more cars than they had friends. This may be hard for you to understand at your age, but I came to believe that my good friend the janitor had a better quality of life than they did.'

The young man spoke: 'So is success an illusion? Is it impossible to carve a business career and still have a life?'

'I have seen some do it, son, but very few. Over the years I've observed the characteristics of those who have achieved

it. I've come to believe that these men and women were truly successful.'

'Is it something I could learn?'

'I'll tell you what I'll do. I'll give you the most radical piece of advice ever given to a student at this fine seat of learning. For the next couple of months or so, come to the library when it's closed. I live in the cottage, just up the drive. Come and visit me. I'll make some coffee for both of us and I'll share with you what my students used to call "Professor Murray's Laws of Success". It'll be kind of nice to do some teaching again. Class starts tomorrow night at 10 sharp.'

For the first time that night Tom saw a huge smile cross the young man's face, 'I'll be there! By the way, my name's Jack.'

Tom let his new student out of the library and watched as he made his way down the road, until the dark of the campus almost swallowed him. Suddenly the young man turned and shouted, 'Hey, Professor, what's your class called?'

The old man smiled and began to make his way back into

the building but then suddenly he stopped and turned. And then he began to chuckle. He squinted hard but the student was long since gone from his sight. That didn't stop him yelling down the hill and into the darkness: 'Jack – we'll call it: "Making It in Business Without Losing in Life!"'

As Jack went back to his flat that night he had no idea that the time he was to spend in Tom Murray's class would change his life. And as we go through the book together I want you, too, to experience the heart of those seven memorable meetings. But there is no tape recording, no video, no written record of the detail of what those two discussed in those autumn evenings all those years ago. However, we do have the professor's seven laws and after each class I will bring you back to the present and interpret them as I believe they affect businesses and individuals today.

Tom Murray is long since dead, and Jack himself is nearing fifty years old, but you may agree with me that the laws are as relevant now as they were then …

Tom opened the door as soon as Jack knocked, and beckoned him in. The room reminded the young man of some bygone age. A small coal fire burned in a grate that was flanked by two old leather armchairs. The seats in both were sunk so low they almost touched the floor. And all around the walls were photographs – of children, and dogs, and one of a young man with his bride on their wedding day. Tom took his new student around each of them, explaining why they were precious to him, and then, lighting a pipe, motioned to one of the armchairs.

'Well, Jack, class begins! Like all the best professors I'm going to give you the final examination question on the first day and spend the rest of the time teaching you how to answer it! Here it is: "What is the heart of real success – how can I find it in my business and my life?"

'And the first lesson's the hardest …'

DON'T SETTLE FOR BEING MONEY RICH – TIME POOR

The
Heart of
Success

DON'T SETTLE FOR BEING
MONEY RICH – TIME POOR

It was a hot – no, sweltering – afternoon in California when I saw it. For the sixtieth time that hour, the early-evening traffic had lurched to a standstill on the freeway coming out of Los Angeles. As I sat there I glanced around at my fellow travellers. In the lane to my left the driver was slumped over the steering wheel in either death or sheer desperation; the business-suited woman in the car in front was alternating between yelling into her mobile and at her kids who were perfecting an art practised by generations of children in the back seats of motor cars – driving their mother crazy; and the man in the Porsche to my right was … well, agitated. He risked losing precious freezing air by lowering his window so that he could lean out and shout at the motorists in front. When he had done this for a while he, too, got on his mobile phone and yelled down that as well. The Porsche and my hire car duetted down the freeway alongside each other for at least five miles and I became fascinated with him. I noticed that he was getting redder and redder and, although I am sure that the climate control on a Porsche Boxster is second to none, this man was perspiring heavily.

So caught up was I in this little pantomime that when the car in front moved forward a couple of yards I was a little slow on the accelerator. Porsche man saw a chance to get into what appeared to be (falsely as it turned out) a faster moving queue and jammed his foot down hard. The small, rocket-like car lurched forward and into the space. And that's when I saw it – on his back bumper – Porsche man's motto: 'He who dies with most toys wins.'

I have often thought of him since. I confess that once or twice I have wondered whether he's still alive, and, if not, what was the prize he won. But most of all I have thought of him because he seems to symbolise what I have come to believe are the new poor. These people have a very high standard of living, but an appalling quality of life. They have every time-saving gadget and yet complain bitterly that 'there aren't enough hours in the day'. They have the very latest in communication technology – you can reach them anywhere, anytime – but they find communicating with those they love almost impossible. They have a second home but they have precious few hours in their first one. They have everything and they have nothing.

I understand that man in the car with his bumper sticker. I sometimes feel I know him. He has left for the office long before his children are awake, and he can't remember the last time he read them a bedtime story. It's not that he wouldn't like to make some of his daughter's ballet performances – it's just that with all the goodwill in the world it seems impossible. And of course he would like just to relax on holiday as his wife begs him to, but 'just one phone call to the office' seems irresistible. He has little time for friends. He's got health cover, he's a member of a fitness club, and his company runs in-house stress-awareness courses, but he's screwed up, he doesn't sleep well, and he's heading for his second heart attack. And of all the issues this character has failed to grasp, none is more damaging than that of 'time poverty' – cash rich, time poor.

The 'time pauper' seems to fit pretty well a definition given by a former chair of the US Chamber of Commerce: 'A well-adjusted executive is one whose intake of pep pills overbalances his consumption of tranquillisers just enough to leave him sufficient energy for the weekly visit to his psychiatrist.' The strange thing about this man is that although he may have qualifications galore, he lives as though he has somehow missed the plot. This is not just my view; a leading headhunter said, 'These days a typical CEO candidate might be forty-eight with a mental age of barely twenty-two and inevitably they will be two sticks short of a bundle. Such are the crazy demands and the need for total support at home and at work.'

Time poverty is hard to spot because often every other part of the life in question seems to be going so very well. This person has a high standard of living, and those they love have every material need provided. The kids get expensive presents at birthdays and Christmas, and attend the best schools. What makes time poverty even harder to spot is that there is often a high level of provision for recreation or leisure activities. The family may go on several holidays a year, there may be a second home in the country, and a family membership of a health and fitness club.

But alongside all this is a hurried, hassled lifestyle that in spite of massive help – au-pairs, fast food, day-care facilities and a myriad of other services – means that the time pauper never quite manages to stay in front. He convinces himself that what he needs is better back-up, and so one of the fastest growing areas for busy executives is companies providing 'concierge services'. These will organise your children's birthday parties or arrange your family photograph album for you. They will provide greeting cards that read, 'Sorry I can't be there to tuck you in tonight.' Services now exist that will provide you with stress-relieving massage at your desk to save you the trip to their consulting rooms. Right behind them is the dentist, willing to replace that lost crown without your moving an inch from your work station. And best of all, the humble shoeshine boy will now come to your office to make sure that even if your head's a little fuzzy, at least your feet look good. Hey, why not have all three services at once? Think of the time that would save! Just relax your shoulders, open your mouth wide and stick your feet out. You're successful!

The latest 'perk' in some of the large London City institutions is a 'lifestyle manager'. According to the publicity they 'cater for high-powered executives who are too busy to organise their lives outside work'. They promise to tend to every need from walking the dog to organising a wedding.

The time pauper has a growing sense as the years go by that they have 'missed it' – that somehow they have been cheated or fooled. They have spent the best part of twenty years rushing around fulfilling the demands of others; they have built up a fair stock of material possessions; but they have a gnawing at their very soul that they have had little time to develop close relationships with those they love, to foster deeper personal development.

Time poverty is tragic because while we strive for 'success' it simultaneously attacks those we care about most. A woman writes:

> *Andy and I were so in love when we got married. It's hard to know when we really grew apart. His job became more and more demanding. He came home so tired he could hardly say hello, let alone tell me about his day or be prepared to be interested in mine. I hated it. And then as the years went by a strange thing happened. I learnt to live without him. It was as if something inside said, 'You're on your own; for your sake and the kids' sake, face it and learn to live with it.' And one day I realised I didn't love him any more. The voice I had longed to hear I now hated. He must have sensed this because, incredibly, he then wanted to talk. But it was too late. It was over.*

The heart of success

What does it mean to be successful? How do we measure it? I recently visited a high-security prison. Some of the people incarcerated within such institutions have, in some ways, been very successful. One man had accumulated more money than most people will see in a lifetime. Moreover, if the rumours were true, he still had it – somewhere – waiting for him when the fifteen-year stretch was over. His wife and family lived in a mansion, his kids went to the best schools and his Lexus was still in the garage. But the price he had paid was just too great.

Now come with me to the City of London and to a law practice. Here the newly qualified make at least £50,000 a year plus bonuses, and the partners stopped counting in thousands long ago. One of the lawyers said to me recently, 'We often have to work into the early hours of the morning and at weekends, but it's not too bad; you can send out for any meal you want and there's a room with a television and a Sony Playstation so you can have a break. There are showers and bedrooms too if we need them.'

Of course there are vast differences in the lives of the two men – one in prison and the other in the law practice – but the main one is that although the lawyer gets let out into the exercise yard a little more often, he is in for forty years, not fifteen.

Some years ago I was attending an international law conference in New York. A senior partner of a large US practice was outlining his strategy for building a thriving business.

'We like our young lawyers to produce 2,500 *chargeable* hours a year,' he said. 'We put living accommodation in the offices because we find that going home spoils their rhythm.'

The chairman turned and said, 'But, Sam, what about burn-out?'

He answered without missing a beat: 'No problem, Larry. If they burn out, we don't want them.'

That's old-hat management thinking. It tells you to take somebody in their early twenties and burn them out by the time they are in their late thirties. They'll have their first heart attack at forty. They'll be off work for four months, come back, have their second heart attack at fifty, retire on grounds of ill health, and then you'll start all over again with a new batch of graduates.

The *Financial Times*, commenting on 'The Quality of Working Life', a report by the Institute of Management,[1] said, 'The results underline the business case for reducing working hours. Stress and burn-out may be brushed aside as "personal problems" but the inefficient use of working hours must be a central concern for any business.'[2]

And even if some of the professionals are missing the point, it appears that their clients are not. Recently the Bass company surprised the London legal world by declaring that in future they would insert into their contracts for legal services a requirement that the lawyers they engaged worked no more than a fifty-hour week. They were prepared to pay £300 an hour, but not for jet-lagged, life-lagged drones.[3]

As we speak of these issues we can smell the fear: 'companies will suffer'; 'profits will plummet'. But perhaps Bass are right. Perhaps innovation, great strategy and forward thinking needs space. It would be ironic if we found that, after all, we could get a healthy balance on the accounts and still live a little.

Two years ago KPMG introduced its values charter.

Most of the ten items hold no surprises. You would expect a global giant that enjoys such success to include elements like, 'We will be proactive and innovative with our clients, and will respond to their needs quickly, efficiently and objectively.' It doesn't come as a shock to read, 'We will support our leaders, encourage our peers and develop our people.' But who would have guessed the next two items?

- We will respect our own and our people's need to balance personal and business life.

- We will learn from our experiences and will take time to enjoy our successes in the company of those we work with.

The closing note says, 'Partners as the leaders of the firm are seen as role models for our people and the wider business community.'

These ideals cannot be implemented overnight, and no doubt living them out is somewhat harder than getting them printed, but at the very least KPMG is putting these issues on the agenda.

Every business needs men and women who will

sometimes work long hours. The really disconcerting aspect is that the 'long-hours drone' does it *irrespective of the need*. This character works long hours as a lifestyle. They have got in early, got home late, and taken work home for as long as they can remember. In other words, their effort bears no relation to times of pressure. They just live that way. They would counter by saying, 'But life is always pressurised in this office.' Of course it is. And for several reasons.

First, many offices simply have a 'jacket over the chair' culture. One London executive told me that in her office you daren't go home at six even if all the work is done. She said, 'There's a macho image that makes you hang around until about nine and go home looking weary.' She went on, 'And if anybody asks you how you are, you never say "Oh, fine!" You say, "Shattered!" I know a financial institution where the two directors both get in at 6 a.m. – unless one is on holiday and then the other gets in at half past eight!'

What many people fail to realise is that the leaders of many departments, firms and organisations are desperately insecure. That's hard to understand because they seem so successful. But these men and women have spent their lives asking the question, 'What do people think of me?' It has driven them to prove themselves in just about every area of their lives. Some of them had it inculcated into them by a parent, probably a father, who constantly judged them on achievement. Some of these people are now the heads of organisations and you would think the proving would be over. But it's only just begun. They now feel they must show that they work harder than anybody else. Mark that well – *harder*. Not necessarily more effectively, or better, and certainly not smarter – but *harder*. And so often *harder* means *longer*.

If they just did this to themselves it wouldn't be so much of a problem but often they create organisations where everybody judges each other on the *appearance* of hard work. In such offices men and women who achieve higher targets, sell more insurance or have higher client billing than their colleagues but who refuse to play the long-hours game are often perceived as being uncommitted. People adamantly refuse to believe their success is because they are working smarter; it's more often put down to the fact that their sector is just easier.

We need new heroes leading our firms and organisations who say, 'Don't tell me how long you work – tell me what you get done.' When engineering boss Vicky King was asked to comment on the long-hours culture she cut straight to the chase, insisting that a fresh, rested dynamo 'could cut through a pile of work like a sushi chef fan-chopping mushrooms'. In her opinion, why reward the guy who takes the longest time to do the job?[4] We need business leaders who will demonstrate that successful people have lives outside the office; that really bright people are those who manage to make their success liberate them, not imprison them in some oak-panelled cell.

The second reason the long-hours culture is so prevalent is a lack of maths ability. Let's go back for a moment to those young lawyers earning £50,000 a year. It seems a lot of money, but is it? Many of those young people are working a fourteen-hour day, six days a week, say for forty weeks a year, which puts their hourly rate at £12.40. A lawyer earning £30,000 a year and working a fifty-hour week is getting in at 8 a.m., going home at 6 p.m., having weekends off and is achieving the same hourly rate. I quite understand that the first characters have more disposable income – the only problem is they've got no time to spend it! When are we going to wake up to the fact that the person who balances income with a lifestyle that allows a little living is the bright one?

I have spent much of my life helping businesses to expand but I have come to believe there is little point in doing so if a higher standard of living brings with it a poorer *quality* of life. In 1999 the legal recruitment agency Bygott Biggs and the solicitors' healthcare charity, Solcare, commissioned a survey of lawyers' working lives. It didn't make comfortable reading:

- 70 per cent were completely exhausted;

- 70 per cent are worried about the amount of work they have to do;

- 67 per cent work long hours to get the job done;

- 30 per cent of male and 20 per cent of female lawyers are drinking to excess;
- Alcohol-related deaths in the legal profession are twice the national average.

On one occasion I asked a company director to describe his lifestyle to me. He said, 'I get into the office at 7.30 a.m. and get home about 9 p.m.'

I asked if he worked on Saturdays and he told me he did. 'What about Sundays?' I enquired.

He said, 'I sometimes go in on Sundays so I can clear the decks for Monday.'

I asked him how long he had been living that way and he replied, 'Almost twenty-seven years.'

Twenty-seven years! And I have no doubt for every week of that time, perhaps every day, he was saying to himself, 'This is just a busy period – life will get a little quieter soon.' But his health is gone, his kids are grown, and somehow he feels cheated.

On another occasion I was involved in advising five business partners; they were each in their early thirties. Again I asked them to describe their lifestyle.

'We start at 7 a.m., finish at 9 p.m. and do that six days a week,' one of them explained.

'And how can I help you?' I asked.

She replied quickly, 'We want to expand.'

'Oh', I said, 'that's easy. You must start at 6 a.m., finish at 10 p.m. and do it seven days a week.'

Another in the group looked up accusingly and said, 'You're laughing at us.'

'Forgive me', I said, 'but my great fear for you all is that when you are forty you will be even wealthier than you are now but will have lived those years as paupers.'

Charles Handy, former oil executive, business economist and professor at London Business School puts it like this:

> *What are we doing to ourselves? ... If the brightest and best amongst us have no time for anything or anyone but themselves and their work and if the*

price of success has to be total immersion in that work ... it is the organization, the customers or the clients who suffer ... Those around us, in turn, start to emulate the hours and, often, the behaviours of those above them ... Work then becomes addictive for us all.[5]

Handy recalls how his wife felt when, many years ago, he himself was working those eighty-hour weeks. She said to him, 'I am happy for you that your work is going so well. I just think you should know that you have become the most boring man I know.'[6]

It may be that you have to work very long hours at the beginning of your career – you are trying to earn your spurs, to impress a little, to get noticed. But try not to make a vocation out of it. I believe we are seeing the beginning of a sea change in this area. Young people especially are declaring that they do not want the 'sell us your soul' philosophy in an employer. Some companies, who want to make themselves more attractive in a tight labour market, are beginning to look at things a little differently. They are realising that a decision to opt out of a long-hours culture is a positive advantage in recruitment and are stating their commitment to reasonable hours in their adverts. The City law firm, D. J. Freeman, quotes one of their trainees in their recruitment brochure: 'One of the reasons I like this firm is its approach to its work. It pulls out all the stops for clients but when things are less hectic nobody is expected to stay late to conform to some macho City image.'

Apparently Tom Peters, the management guru, claims to fly anything up to a million miles a year. As a result he often gets asked about work/life balance. He told *Real Business* magazine that it is 'a crime not to be engaged with your work'. But he admits to some doubts over the long-hours culture: 'Am I happy that I've missed too many of my kids' school games days? No.' However, he doesn't seem to have too many doubts saying, 'Are we happy that Winston Churchill missed a few of his kids' soccer games during the war? Yes – I'm glad that Mr Churchill worked twenty-six hours a day during the war.'

I'm glad too. However, even if those troubled times

were filled with frenetic activity, the great man had a quality that most modern business leaders seem to lack: *he managed to notice when the war had finished.*

I have some sympathy for the small boy who said to his mother, 'Why does my father come home later than all the other kids' dads?'

His mother said, 'Well, because he can't finish all his work in the normal time.'

The child paused for a moment and said, 'Why don't they put him in a slower class?'

EXECUTIVE BRIEFING

Danger signs at work

❏ You're still up to your neck in your last project. Nobody could possibly do it as well.

❏ You work longer hours than anybody else.

❏ You resent colleagues who seem to have found some balance.

❏ You take work home every night and on weekends.

❏ Your schedule has no time for creative and strategic thinking.

❏ You are impatient or edgy with colleagues and family when pressurised.

❏ You find it hard to delegate.

❏ You find it hard to accept even gentle and constructive criticism.

❏ Your responses to crises are emotional and disproportionate.

Danger signs in your body

❏ Increasing headaches;

❏ Itching skin;

❏ Prolonged exhaustion;

❏ Stomach complaints;

❏ Often being ill on holiday;

❏ Increasing irritability;

❏ Difficulty in concentrating;

❏ Getting annoyed at the smallest things – for example, if the petrol pump doesn't dispense quickly enough!

Danger signs in your family

- ☐ Your kids have stopped telling you about their problems and achievements.

- ☐ Your partner feels excluded – you don't row so much as simply not talk any more – what one husband called 'a creeping separateness'.

- ☐ You are often late for important family events.

- ☐ Your finances are out of control.

- ☐ You believe yourself when you say, 'Soon we'll have more time.'

Danger signs among your friends

- ❏ You usually have meals out in your business clothes.

- ❏ You have lost touch with the world around you – current affairs, sport, arts, movies.

- ❏ Your eyes glaze over during normal conversation and only sparkle when you talk about work.

- ❏ Your friends stop calling.

- ❏ In short: you're a bore.

Getting Back on Track

❏ Consider whether your quality of life has deteriorated in direct relation to an increase in your standard of living. Most people trade their time for money. Is it possible you have gone too far in that direction and need to reduce income or expenditure in order to allow a less pressurised lifestyle? Don't stop doing things; just do some different, perhaps less expensive, things. In other words, 'buy some time.' It could involve some big decisions – size of house, type of car, numbers of holidays. Even, perish the thought, people thinking you've fallen on hard times – 'They used to change their car every year!'

❏ Consider the possibility that your long hours have more to do with your need to be recognised as 'hard-working' than the job in hand. Resist the temptation to stay late to prove a point. The people who are most free feel they have nothing to prove. One bright CEO used to say to new staff, *'In this organisation it's not the hours you put in that count – it's what you put into the hours.'*

❏ Practise saying 'no' in front of a mirror. Imagine every 'yes' as a coin in those arcade games that build up with others near the edge and one day fall off! One manager put it like this: 'I stand looking out of my office window frozen in time. I don't know what to do next.'

❏ Do your part in creating a work culture that honours achievement rather than long hours.

❏ Don't settle long-term in a company that demands your soul or tries to buy your years with money or power.

❏ Establish a 'life board' – three people you respect who will give counsel and direction.

'Try to get here on time, son – my bedtime's fast approaching.'

Jack mumbled an apology, slid deep into the old leather chair and then saw the twinkle in the old boy's eyes.

'I'm kidding you, Jack – one of the few advantages of old age is you seem to need less sleep, not more. Just my luck to be able to stay awake all night when my body can't dance.'

Tom walked across the room and pointed to an old photograph that hung near the mantelpiece. 'Do you recognise that, son?'

The young man answered in a heartbeat, 'Yes, it's St Paul's Cathedral.'

'You know, Jack, when it was being built, Sir Christopher Wren, the architect, was walking around the site one day and came upon a young apprentice carrying a hod. Wren asked the boy what he was doing. "I'm just carrying bricks, sir," came the reply. "No", said Wren, "you are building a cathedral." The great architect understood the importance of the law we are going to study together tonight ...'

LAW NUMBER TWO

BELIEVE THAT THE JOB YOU DO MAKES A DIFFERENCE

The Heart of Success

BELIEVE THAT THE JOB YOU DO
MAKES A DIFFERENCE

My father was a postman. He joined what was then the General Post Office as a fourteen-year-old boy repairing the wiring at the top of telegraph poles, and went on to deliver letters for the rest of his working life. He was bright – very bright – and when he came back from the Second World War the authorities in the postal service asked him to train for management. But something had happened to my father in the war – what, we'll never know. He wouldn't talk about it. The only clue we ever got was when, after he died, I was sifting through his papers and found his army discharge book. In it was a commendation from his commanding officer for outstanding service under the most difficult circumstances. My father was in the Royal Signals and the smart money is on his being a wireless operator behind enemy lines. But whatever it was, when he got home in 1945 he didn't want any hassle. He wasn't looking for glory, he just wanted to provide for his family the best way he could and he wanted to deliver letters.

My father sometimes worked a night shift, as a sorter of mail. One of my abiding memories is of him getting ready for work just as I tried to extend bedtime. In those days we didn't have a bathroom, all the washing there was – whether dishes, clothes or bodies – was done in the large stone kitchen sink, and so I could watch him. First he would lay out his uniform, and then he would shave, wash and, finally, he would clean his shoes.

My father's shoes always shone. One day when I was about eight or nine, I caught him cleaning the *underside* of them. I said, 'Don't do that, Dad – it's a waste of time – nobody will ever know.'

He looked up at me and said, '*I'll* know.'

The years went by and the time came when I had to leave the small junior school where all my friends from our street went, and join the grammar school. It was another world to me. I remember once the teacher asked us to shout out what our fathers did for a living. The boy next to me yelled out, 'company director.' I can remember whispering, 'postman' as quietly as I could.

One night when my father was getting ready for work I interrupted him: 'Don't you ever get bored of just pushing letters through doors?'

If I hurt him he didn't show it. He said, 'Son, your father delivers the Royal Mail.' He made it sound as if the Queen herself had asked him to do it. 'People rely on me – businesses, armies and police forces, friends and relatives from overseas – I deliver all their letters. You should come with me some day and see somebody waiting at their door to see if I've got a letter for them. It may be about a job they've been hoping for or from a daughter they haven't heard from for a while, or perhaps just a birthday card. No, son, I don't get bored.'

My father believed in the value of what he did.

Recently I was invited to be a keynote speaker at the

annual conference of the Life Insurance Association. The delegates arrived at that conference battered. For the previous year they had been hammered in the media (sometimes with justification) over mis-selling. It was a fascinating occasion. Stephen Horswell, the president that year, had put together a team of speakers, none of whom had the brief to help those delegates close a sale. There were no seminars on what to do if the client says, 'Thanks for the advice – I'd like to think about it.' No workshops entitled, 'Cold calling – ten tips to success'. Instead the programme was designed to help these men and women believe in themselves again and, while acknowledging where the industry needed to change, to begin to believe again in the intrinsic worth of the job they did – to rediscover their pride.

I reminded the audience that during the Gulf War twelve soldiers lost their lives in a helicopter accident. The insurance company paid out on each of those men's lives even though the proposal forms for life cover had not been received, let alone the contracts underwritten. They should be proud of that.

Many companies need to rediscover a sense of

pride in what they do. Hans Raunsing, the Swedish billionaire who invented Tetrapack packaging, talks constantly not about packaging but about providing fresh, uncontaminated vitamins for children around the world. My mind goes to a large pharmaceutical company that called in consultants to help it develop its staff and increase employee motivation and loyalty. They were ready to discuss salary packages, holiday enhancements, cars and a host of other fringe benefits. The managing director gave the consultant carte-blanche. But this was no ordinary consultant. She didn't begin with packages, she began with people. She told them to erect huge posters in the reception area, at the security gates, in the corridors and staff canteens – all over the offices – of real people whose lives had been saved by the medicines that the company produced. Before salary, holidays and the company car – and whether they were scientists, typists or office cleaners – these people needed to believe again in the value of the job they did.

My father would have approved of that. He believed that every job had worth and therefore you should do it as well as you possibly can. I have seen him in driving rain trying to keep his letters dry. It brought him satisfaction to do it well.

It was one of the directors of a major airline who said, 'Coffee stains on the flip-down tray prove to our passengers that we don't do our engine maintenance properly.' That is completely illogical – and utterly true. I know; I fly a lot. If I'm in the toilet of a 747 and the flush doesn't work I immediately begin to think about the other bits of machinery: 'Are those oxygen masks really up there? I've never seen one yet.' I don't understand reverse thrusters or intricate braking systems and my grasp of undercarriages is limited to knowing by the clunking sound whether they are up or down. But flushes I understand; I've used them, repaired them; I even own a couple.

My father and the director of the airline company would have got along just fine. They both understood one of the fundamentals of business life: if the customer gets the message that you don't care – whether it's by unreturned phone calls, late delivery dates or keeping them waiting in reception for an hour – then pretty soon that customer will begin to doubt the quality of your core business. You may be the best accountant in the Western world but unless your client believes you are, then it's a secret between you and your diary.

I was lecturing in Moscow when I got the news that my father was dying. The Russian authorities rushed me through Moscow airport; a British Airways flight into Heathrow was slightly delayed and I just managed to catch it. And as that plane made its way across the night sky above Europe my mind was going back over my memories of this man: things I would have liked to have said to him and a couple I wish I hadn't. But above all I was trying again to understand him.

When I landed it was in the early hours of the morning and I was again rushed through immigration and customs. A driver was waiting to take me to my father. I got in the car and asked him, 'How's my dad?'

'I'm sorry,' he said. 'Your father died a couple of hours ago.'

I remember walking into his room and looking at

him. I almost expected him to say some old familiar phrase, and yet as I looked at him he was still in so many ways an enigma to me. He was poor and yet he was never in debt; he had few possessions and yet he was the most content man I have ever met – and every single day of his life he cleaned his shoes.

And my father delivered letters – for forty-six years. In all that time he had only eleven days' absence due to sickness. When he retired the Queen gave him a medal; it was for delivering the Royal Mail.

The best way I can explain it is to say that my father had *dignity*. You can't buy that. You can't guarantee it by education, or social status. My father was proud to be a postman; he believed that the job he did made a difference in peoples' lives. And because he had that dignity he owed it to himself to do whatever job he did as well as he could, and with all his heart.

That's why my father cleaned his shoes.

The power of trust

My father believed in honesty too. I quite understand that the work he did wasn't full of daily ethical dilemmas or ferocious negotiations such as characterise some businesses, but I happen to believe that he would have behaved much the same even in those – perhaps to his detriment. He believed that if he lost his integrity, he lost his greatest asset – his character. And character mattered to him. Mother Teresa said, 'Small things are indeed small, but faithfulness in small things is a great thing.'

Some time ago one of New York's leading executive search firms conducted a survey of CEOs of the top 100 companies in the New York area. The object of the survey was fascinating. It did not seek to measure business acumen, or even ability to handle clients or personnel. It sought to measure *character*. They asked these leaders what character traits they most valued, and which should be nurtured in the new generation of the USA's leaders.

This is how these men and women voted:

1　Never compromise on matters of principle nor standards of excellence, even on minor issues.

2 Be persistent and never give up.

3 Have a vision of where you are going and communicate it often.

4 Know what you stand for, set high standards, and don't be afraid to take on tough problems despite the risk.

5 Spend less time managing and more time leading. Lead by example.

6 Bring out the best in others. Hire the best people you can find, then delegate authority and responsibility, but stay in touch.

7 Have confidence in yourself and in those around you; trust others.

8 Accept blame for failures and credit others with success. Possess integrity and personal courage.

There is no shortage of seminar material, books or vidcos that proclaim thcir ability to producc effective managers. They cover motivation, strategic thinking, team building and a host of other 'buzz' topics. But are these the most crucial elements? I would guess that a survey of British companies would discover similar findings to those on the other side of the pond. People want leaders they can trust.

I'm honestly not sure whether those whose word you can depend upon and whose integrity you take for granted get better jobs, are better salespeople or hit higher fee targets. The truth is that duplicity and manipulation produce rewards, otherwise they wouldn't be so attractive. But I am sure that people who live like that are forever wondering when their turn will come to be deceived, when one of the people they have abused will come back into their life, whether any of the little people they have ripped off will ever become 'big players' and seek revenge.

And I am also sure that while for a time the people who are 'hard-nosed', 'cut-throat', 'dog-eat-dog' kind of animals are admired by some, when they fall, their erstwhile admirers are nowhere to be seen. If a man or woman of integrity loses their success they still have their character, but the only thing that makes a charlatan worth knowing is his success; he had better not lose it.

Frank Davidson was one of the most successful contract managers for a major construction company. Frank's speciality, for which he was often brought in, was to pull a project that was fast becoming a liability back into profit. Imagine that the company was contracted to build an opera house. It was a design-and-build contract so the firm was responsible for the whole shooting match – including the need to come in on the nose of a fixed price. It was a hard commission to win, and by the time they had signed the contract they were already having second thoughts, but by now the PR machine was rolling and somebody at the top demanded they proceed though they yelled down the phone, 'You had better bring this thing in on price.'

It went badly from the start. The geological report turned out to be a not-very-accurate guess, and the clay they had priced the job on seemed to turn very quickly into granite. They spent ten weeks blasting before anybody thought of laying foundations. There's an old saying that once things start going wrong they will continue to do so in an exponential curve. They did; from the demands of an unreasonable fire officer, to local protest groups that actually occupied five JCBs and two cranes for ten days, to rain that didn't stop for a month. Three months to the end of the contract and they were staring in the face both a loss and public humiliation. Enter Frank and his fail-safe rescue programme.

Frank demands that every contract with their small company subcontractors – whether for electrics, seating, curtaining or fire safety equipment – be scrutinised. Faults are to be found in their jobs even if there are none. His people are experts – they can come up with a snag list a mile long on Michelangelo's ceiling in the Sistine Chapel. The next step is to stop all payments to these subcontractors. There have already been hefty deductions from the monthly invoices these 'subbies' have put in and so now these 'small people' have a dilemma. Do they walk off-site and sue, or keep going to the end in the hope of getting paid when the job is completed? Many of them are operating on small margins, with a bank manager on their back, and three kids and a mortgage to support. Such people have no choice. They almost always keep going.

When the job is completed, Frank tells his people to find more faults in the subcontractors' work and pay a tiny proportion of what is owed. The owners of these small businesses are beside themselves. A few take a day off work and visit a solicitor, but when the lawyer takes a look at the snag list on their work, and a glance at the size of the company they are up against, he urges them against even contemplating litigation. In homes across the area, people explain to their partners why they can't afford to pay the mortgage that month. Six weeks later their tiny companies go into voluntary liquidation. Big Builder plc settles at a fraction of the real cost with the liquidator.

The sad thing about that scenario is that it occurs in one way or another every day of the week, and the really sad thing is that in some companies it has come to be a way of life.

But then there is a twist in the tale. News has got out that Frank has been fired. Apparently some invoices went in that couldn't be reconciled and Frank was accused of taking back-handers off some contractors. He protested his innocence. And in truth he may have been guiltless, but Frank had spent all his life ripping people off and, sure, he was a heck of a contracts manager but, 'You couldn't trust him further than you could throw him.' On his first day at the dole office Frank meets Clive Harries, an electrician he had driven out of business three years ago.

Frank doesn't go out much these days.

I like the fact that in the US CEOs' list of top qualities, 'integrity' and 'courage' are linked. Character often needs courage. There is an inherent strain in us all to cover our backs, to pin the blame on somebody else, to 'look after number one'. And therefore character will often cost us. It will mean you own up when you've got it wrong, rather than shift the blame to a colleague. It will mean you don't tell the clients that the contract is in the post or your creditor that his cheque is on its way, when the first is waiting to be drafted, and the second is waiting for cash flow to improve. Very simply it will mean that you tell the truth. You do that when it makes life easier for you and when it costs you, and even when to tell a 'white lie' would hurt nobody.

Anita Roddick, founder of the Body Shop, put it like this:

> *I am still looking for the modern-day equivalent of those Quakers who ran successful businesses, made money because they offered honest products and treated their people decently, worked hard themselves, spent honestly, saved honestly, gave honest value for their money, put back more than they took out and told no lies.* [7]

The Quakers believed that when you live so that your character matters more to you than success, you discover that people trust you. Bosses will trust you, as will those who work for you. Even some customers will trust you! And, in the long run, trust pays dividends. They may not be as large as if you'd manipulated, lied and short-changed others – but they will be sweeter.

And, unlike Frank, you'll still be able to get out a little.

EXECUTIVE BRIEFING

Believe the job you do makes a difference

❏ Does your company need to rediscover a pride in what it does?

❏ Does the most junior person in your organisation understand what you do, how you do it, and why?

❏ How could the value of what you do be communicated across the workforce?

'Coffee stains on the flip-down tray prove to our passengers we don't do our engine maintenance properly.'

❏ What is the equivalent of 'coffee stains' in your business?

❏ **Consider adopting a company charter**

Company Charter

1. Every year we will reinvest part of our skills, resources and vision into the community.

2. We will endeavour to instil in our people the intrinsic worth of the job they do.

3. We will take on board our employees as whole people. In so far as resources allow, we will support them in their lives outside of the work environment. We realise it is foolish to say, 'Leave your home troubles at the office door.'

4. We will help our people discover and play to their strengths. We will remind managers that sometimes special gifts are found in unusual places.

5. We undertake to operate with integrity towards our clients, our staff and our colleagues.

6. We will not tolerate a long-hours culture for its own sake. There will be periods when we will need to work harder, longer, and with more intensity. At such times we expect that each of us will make sacrifices in personal and family life. But we do not accept that as a lifestyle.

7. We will try to remember that generally people don't leave jobs, they leave supervisors. We will find and develop managers who inspire respect and loyalty.

In short, we'll be a company that's worth getting out of bed for.

Trust and integrity

❑ Is it possible that over a period of time your company has come to operate in a way that compromises the integrity of the company and its people?

If so, then are there any steps that could be taken to re-establish trust between employees and management, with clients or customers, and with suppliers?

❑ Successful, long-term leaders base their relationships on trust:

- Of their character;
- Of their competence.

Stephen Covey talks of trust having to be earned. He suggests that each of us has a 'trust account' with another person. We make character deposits by doing what we say we will do. We make competency deposits by doing it well. We also make withdrawals and sometimes our account becomes overdrawn. Sometimes the other person will 'close' it; in other words, they have lost all trust in us.[8]

As he walked up the hill towards Tom's home, Jack wondered what it was that made this man so different from almost anybody he'd ever met. It was true that he was wise, and for sure he was kind, but it was something else. It came to him as the old boy opened the door and greeted him: Tom made him feel special – as if he had all the time in the world for just him.

The professor smiled widely. 'Before we make the coffee I've a question for you: "What's the fastest way to success?"'

The young man grimaced; he needed the caffeine to get his brain in gear. 'Is it hard work?' He could see from the look on Tom's face that it wasn't. 'What about perseverance?' It seemed not.

'Son, the fastest way to succeed is to find what you're good at and find somebody to let you do it! It's the next law...'

PLAY TO YOUR STRENGTHS – FIND YOUR FACTOR X

The Heart of Success

Play to Your Strengths –
Find Your Factor X

Most of us have read George Orwell's *Animal Farm* but just in case you last studied it in the fourth form let me remind you how it ends. In short: the pigs have taken over the place, the humans are out, and the animals are running the show. If you cast your mind back you'll also recall that the big surprise is that the pigs have learnt to walk on two legs and now live in the farmhouse. Worse still, they are now every bit as repressive and exploitive as the farmer who used to run the place. But here's the big question that Orwell didn't answer – based on the premise that none of us have ever seen a farm, successful or otherwise, run by pigs – what happened?

The truth is they blew it. From a pig on the front

cover of *Time* magazine to a company in liquidation in less time than it takes to cook bacon. It's true they employed the very best consultants, had the latest technology, and a business plan that would have had Warren Buffett drooling to get a slice of the action – but the farm failed. Why? Well, to find out let's drop in on a meeting of the board. The date is 5 June 1953. There are twelve pigs around the table resting their trotters on the walnut, all smoking Havanas and coughing badly. Frank Trotter, the CEO, is speaking.

'Now turn to number six on the agenda – advertising. Will somebody tell me why, after a whole year, we still haven't got the sign that advertises the farm fixed to the top of the big tree?'

Chris Bacon, head of marketing, shuffles uneasily in his seat. 'Sir, that sign has been ready for over a year. I have yelled, threatened, and begged maintenance to get it fixed to the tree, but they keep coming up with excuses.'

Carl Porker, head of operations, already has his answer ready and delivers it with resolve. 'It's not that we haven't tried. But every time we try to get the turkey to climb the tree with a fixing line, he falls off. Just last week we got him halfway up but then he got a claw caught in the bark and practically broke his neck. We've had him part way up that tree every day for a whole year.'

Susan Snouter, head of animal resources and training, chips in. 'I have had that turkey on more tree-climbing courses and seminars than you've had mudbaths. But we believe he just lacks motivation. I hate to say it of a colleague, but he just doesn't seem to have it.'

The pigs allowed only one non-trotter into the meeting – the company secretary – and even he, the owl, got in only because he could take notes. He had never before had the courage to speak out: 'Sir, forgive my interrupting, but could I say something just this once?'

Twelve pairs of pig eyes turned on him.

'If you must,' said the CEO.

'Sir, why not send the squirrel up with the line? Everybody knows the turkey's a turkey at it.'

The CEO didn't answer at once. He simply stood and toddled towards the owl. He was a little unsteady on two trotters and once or twice had to grasp the table for support, but eventually he made the whole length of the room and was eyeball to eyeball with the company secretary.

'Do you see what I have just done?' he screamed at the unfortunate bird.

'Yes, sir – you walked – upright.'

'No, Owl, I didn't just walk upright. I *achieved*. And that's what this board believes in. We're a no-limits organisation, Owl. The turkey will climb that tree. Now get out!'

Owl closed the boardroom door quietly behind him and, head hung low, made his way across the farmyard. In the distance he could see the cows shuffling uneasily as if afraid to break the eggs they were hatching, the chickens were guarding the corn-store, and his best friend the squirrel was just going under for the third time in yet another swimming lesson on the pond. And as he passed the great oak a turkey fell on his head.

The key to the heart of success for both individuals and companies is to discover what I call Factor X, and then be set free to use it. Factor X is that ability in a man or a woman that is a natural strength – it sets them apart from the pack. The problem is that in life we are dogged by people who want us to be just like them or, in companies, by managers who say, 'This is the way we've always done it.' It may be that our parents have pressurised us to take the career that, given the chance, they themselves would have loved to pursue. The problem is that it is *their* dream, not ours. I am convinced that most people have never had the opportunity to consider, let alone discover, what their natural strengths are.

These are not easy issues. The vast majority of employees in this country work for small organisations of fewer than twenty people. The need here is for people to 'muck in', often in an effort to simply keep the ship afloat. The last thing a director needs is an audiotypist who is spending her whole day dreaming of being a sales representative. But that said it makes sense to consider whether among our staff we have some gifts that are just waiting to be discovered. It's pretty sobering, for example, to meet the head of sales of our major competitor – for whom our previous secretary now works – and hear that the person who used to type our letters actually has an incredible gift and has just won the annual sales prize for the third year running.

So often when companies discover a glimmer of Factor X in a member of staff they first try to control it, then regulate it, and eventually extinguish it. They say, 'She's a rebel', or 'It's not policy to do it that way', or 'That's not in her job description.' But if you are fortunate enough to have somebody in your business with Factor X – change the job to suit them.

I have seen companies killed by their refusal to allow Factor X to blossom. I have often been asked to help professional practices develop new business. There may be fifteen partners around the boardroom table. This firm is dying on the vine – desperate to break into new markets. I begin by saying, 'I know none of you but I'll bet my shirt there's somebody around this table who is brilliant at new-business development. This person builds relationships, they create opportunities, they dream marketing, they only have to walk down the high street to come back with a hatful of work.' Fourteen heads turn and look at Laura, who blushes slightly. I drop my gaze to scan the departmental fee targets and ask, 'Then why have you given her £150,000 of audit costs to bring in? Set her free.'

Martin, one of the partners who never wanted to bring in a consultant anyway, sees this as his moment, 'But we haven't got anybody else to do her work – we can't afford to do it.' At this point I rarely have to say anything else because normally there will be a chorus from the other partners – these people can see the answer, they just needed somebody to turn the light on – '*Martin, we can't afford not to.*'

What a tragedy it is when nobody takes the time to help us discover our Factor X, and what desperate lives many of us are condemned to as we try to be what others want us to be.

A friend of mine is the UK managing director of a

company that is dedicated to helping people discover and develop their strengths. She has travelled the world working with many of the largest companies and helping them to develop the natural gifting of their employees and management, but just recently she faced one of her most challenging assignments. Her daughter Sarah, aged fifteen, had returned home after a consultation with a schools' careers officer. She had been asked what she wanted to do when she left school. Sarah had replied immediately, 'I want to sell.' She said she couldn't have created a look of greater displeasure on the teacher's face if she had offered streetwalking in the Bronx. She felt the need to redeem herself and quickly moved on, '… or do drama – I sometimes think I'd like to be a drama teacher.' This was met with much greater approval and Sarah was sent home with a sackful of literature on what she had to do to reach this worthy goal.

That night my friend saw the look of despair on her daughter's face as she came home from school and put the coffee on as Sarah unpacked her experience of choosing a vocation.

'Sarah, do you like drama?'

'Mum, I *love* drama.'

'Do you like kids?'

'Mum, I can't stand kids.'

And it was at that moment that the managing director got her own offspring as a client. She put Sarah through their skills discovery programme. The results were a surprise to nobody except a careers advisor. Sarah was born to sell. When my friend related this event to me she said, 'I not only saved Sarah from generations of kids. I saved generations of kids from Sarah!'

Wayne Gretzky is probably the greatest ice hockey player who has ever lived: sixty-one National Hockey League records, including all-time goals, assists and points, nine Most Valuable Player awards and a host of other honours. When Gretzky was at the height of his career he could make some of the greatest defence men in the world look as though they'd taken to the ice for the first time that day. I asked a sports psychologist to what she attributed his success. She said, 'The man can see the rink from above.' I asked her to elaborate. She said, 'Most ice hockey players have 20- to 25-degree peripheral vision. Gretzky has forty degrees. At times it's as if he's suspended above the play and can read the whole surface. Whoever put Gretzky together wanted him to play ice hockey.' That fits; when asked what he thought was the secret of his success, Gretzky said simply, 'I skate where the puck is *going* to be.' I asked the sports psychologist if we could coach this level of intuition into new players. She didn't stop laughing for an hour.

Imagine for a moment that when the three-year-old Gretzky is on his way to his first ice hockey lesson his father has second thoughts. 'Ice hockey is a rough game,' muses Gretzky senior. 'Let's try piano first.' He swerves the car away from the rink and towards Mrs Arkwright's School for Young Musicians. Gretzky endures those lessons for a whole year. He is probably the worst piano player in the history of the instrument. He pleads with his father to release him but his father says, 'No – my father always wanted me to be a pianist.' At the first concert Wayne's father waits patiently for his boy to perform. And finally the moment comes and Wayne Gretzky, blessed by heaven with 40-degree peripheral vision, Wayne Gretzky who was born to bend a puck around a defender from forty yards and into a gap just six feet wide and four feet high, Gretzky the 'Great One', begins Mozart's Piano Concerto No. 25 in C Major. As Wayne fumbles and crashes his way through one of the most beautiful pieces of music ever written, far above the earth two cries of anguish penetrate the night sky. One is from the angel who helped put this genius of the ice together and the second is from … Mozart.

Some time ago I saw a 'motivational poster.' It read, 'There is no "I" in TEAM.' Well whoever designed it got the spelling right but the philosophy will kill a company dead in the water. Great teams are made up of brilliant individuals who are allowed to play to their strengths. I have yet to see Alex Ferguson, manager of Manchester United Football Club, demand that his goalkeepers practise bending a ball around a wall. Who would do that when they've got Beckham? Great captains and great managers have the same skill: *they create team spirit while allowing individual brilliance to shine*.

How can companies effectively reward those who have special strengths? By giving them more opportunity to *use* those strengths. If you have a leading salesman you may think you reward him by pulling him off the road and making him a manager. But we somehow have to create a culture that will make him feel valued while allowing him to go on doing what he is uniquely gifted to do. *Don't give him a bigger office; give him a bigger challenge*.

There is nothing more tragic than seeing somebody clinging to a promotion with white knuckles that in reality is stifling their real gift and driving everybody crazy. The problem is caused because so often companies measure success in such a limited way. But great managers *create* ladders. They realise that sometimes you have to shape the job around the person. In other words: *develop your strengths – appoint staff according to your weaknesses*.

Anita Roddick remembers her mother saying to her, 'Anita, be special; be anything but mediocre.'[9] In the film *Chariots of Fire* Eric Liddell, who won the

Olympic gold, said, 'God made me fast and when I run I feel his pleasure.' Liddell had found his Factor X. I believe that each of us has a responsibility to help at least one person find theirs. That is true whether we are parents, friends or CEOs of companies. People are our greatest strength. Our competitors can copy our technology, but they can't copy our people. And people allowed to play to their strengths are an awesome force.

In the film *Patton*, George C. Scott, playing the hero, is looking with binoculars down a long valley. He is watching as his arch-enemy Rommel moves his tanks into position at the other end of the valley. Patton attacks him on the flanks and experiences a decisive victory. As he muses after the battle he says, 'Rommel, you old fox – I read your book.'

Patton had taken the time to understand his adversary. In business it's just as important to 'read the book' of our colleagues, our staff – our people – to understand why and how they act as they do. And, if possible, to read our own book too.

You and I will never discover the heart of success until we know our strengths and find those who allow us to play to them. But hurry, time is short. Quentin Crisp was right. 'It's no good running a pig farm badly for thirty years while saying, "Really I was meant to be a ballet dancer." By that time pigs will be your style.'

EXECUTIVE BRIEFING

For individuals

Most people have spent less time considering what their strengths might be than cleaning their tennis shoes. Embark today on a research programme ... on you!

Have a cup of coffee with somebody whose opinion you value and whose confidentiality you respect. Ask the following questions:

- ❏ What do you consider to be my main gift or skill?

- ❏ Can you think of any steps I could take to use that skill more effectively?

- ❏ Am I in the right organisation?

- ❏ Where do you feel I could be of most value in my organisation?

- ❏ Is there a skill that my organisation needs and that I could acquire?

Ask yourself:

- ❏ If I could choose, what job or role would I love to try?

- ❏ What tasks come easily to me?

- ❏ Is most of my time spent doing things that play to my strengths?

- ❏ How important is it to me to have the opportunity to do what I am best at? What if it meant forgoing career progression and financial rewards for the chance to do it?

For companies

- ❏ Do I have any process that would allow me to discover people's hidden strengths?

- ❏ Has our reward system of promotion inadvertently moved people away from their Factor X?

Life is not easy for any of us. But what of that? We must have perseverance and, above all, confidence in ourselves. We must believe that we are gifted for something, and that this thing, at whatever cost, must be attained.

Marie Curie

Jack sat patiently while Tom struggled to light his pipe. Finally the professor peered up at him through a cloud of smoke. 'Got a basic business question for you, son. Who said, "You can have any colour so long as it's black"?'

The student answered with all the eagerness of a fourth-grader, 'Henry Ford!'

'Correct. Now let me tell you something you didn't know about him. When Ford began he invited a time and motion person in to evaluate his operation. As he showed the consultant around the complex they came upon a man sitting in an armchair with his feet on the mantelpiece, smoking a pipe. Ford said, "Hands off him – he has made me, and saved me, more money than all the others put together."

The professor sucked on his pipe as if to identify himself with Henry's armchair advisor and said, 'We need more of them, son – we need to find the dreamers. Get your pencil out and write this one down ...'

BELIEVE IN
THE POWER OF
DREAMS

The
Heart of
Success

BELIEVE IN THE
POWER OF DREAMS

When I was a small boy my sisters used to make fun of me. They would call me 'the dreamer'. They were right. I wasn't good at school, and never did make the football team, but I loved to sit and dream. Sometimes I would sit in front of the coal fire that burned in our living-room and get lost in the labyrinths of glowing ash and flame, and just – imagine. I can't remember now what captured my mind at those times but I wouldn't mind betting it was coming top in maths, scoring the winning goal in a football game or, in later years, getting a date with Carol Perkins who lived on the corner of our street and who was unassailable unless you were five years older than she was and owned a motorbike.

I'm now forty years on from the days when I would sit in front of that coal fire and dream, and yet I wish I could recapture the child who did just that. The problem with most people in business is that they have stopped dreaming. It was their dreams that inspired them and caused them to scribble ideas on the back of envelopes, bore their friends to death, and frustrate their bank managers with ideas that seemed impossible. But now their businesses are established. Their friends may admire them, and their bank managers may send them diaries at Christmas, but they have stopped dreaming. They are now administrators. It seems to me that if Richard Branson has got anything right in his business life it's that he has never grown up. He spends half his time dreaming.

The most famous dream in the world was held in the mind of Dr Martin Luther King: 'I have a dream my four little children will one day live in a nation where they will not be judged by the colour of their skin but by the content of their character. I have a dream today.' His dream inspired millions to make a difference even when a whole world screamed at them, 'Yours is an impossible dream.' But dreams change things – companies, individuals and even societies. God has created us to have dreams. Robert Browning wrote, 'Ah, but a man's reach should exceed his grasp, or what's a heaven for?'

And yet the very word 'dreamer' implies somebody who never gets things done. That's no excuse to stop dreaming. But what we must do is to combine the power of the dream with some rather more down-to-earth strategies that translate wishes into reality. If you've had dreams but never seen them fulfilled, the next few pages could change your life. If you've got a 'dreamer' in your company, don't fire them; instead, employ the following strategies. In doing so you will unleash one of the most powerful forces ever known – the combination of the dreamer and the dream-catcher.

Every dreamer needs a dream-catcher

Hanging on my study wall, and right in front of me as I type this book, is something that looks rather like a large fishing net. It is a band of circular metal, with mesh of two sizes attached to it. Feathers hang down around the edges. I had heard of these but never seen one until recently when I walked into a tiny shop that sells goods from the North American Indian Reservations. There it was, hanging from the ceiling: the dream-catcher.

We all know the dangers for dreamers. They are likely to walk with their heads in the clouds; they may take foolish risks; their dreams may be not only unlikely but downright impossible. It was one thing for the ugly duckling to dream of being a swan, but he could have dreamt all his life of being a pink flamingo and never had a chance of making it. And for all those reasons the dreamer needs to have at least one person they can share their dream with, who will encourage them, sometimes bring them a little nearer earth, and occasionally tell them they are in 'pink flamingo' mode. The book of Proverbs says, 'There is safety in many counsellors.' It's normally foolish and always arrogant to believe that nobody else could possibly understand, or help us to catch our dreams.

But it is vital that the people that we take into our

confidence are men and women of *vision* – sometimes they are called 'can do' people. I call them *'dream-catchers'*. When they see a mountain in the way they don't say, 'We must turn back.' They ask, 'How can we get over it, around it or get rid of it?' Dream-*killers* say, 'That is the biggest mountain I have ever seen. I bet people have died trying to get over that thing – probably some this very afternoon.'

Many people who have never been able to fulfil their dreams have just shared them with the wrong people. You may be one of those. You ran to your boss, friends or family full of the new idea, bursting with the possibility of the dream, but little did you know that the bucket of cold water was already waiting behind the door. There have been times in my life where I have been part of the answer to people realising their dreams and sadly occasions when I have been part of the problem. Let me tell you about one of the latter.

I stood with a man and his wife in front of a plot of land. He was disabled; in fact he had been in a wheelchair for over ten years. They were drawing social security benefit. They told me they had a dream to build a holiday centre for disabled people. He said, 'I want to build an adventure park for disabled kids in the grounds. Kids in wheelchairs need to take risks too – even if once in a while they fall out of the wheelchair.'

In my view this dream was well into the 'pink flamingo' category and I warned them about having unrealistic goals. They were disappointed but polite and thanked me for my time and advice. Perhaps I'd annoyed them but the second they left my office they got started on their dream.

She got a job as a nurse; he began making furniture and selling it to friends and family. Eventually they bought a tiny terraced house that was, in estate agent's language, 'in need of some modernisation'. They lived on a pittance and used every penny to improve their new property. They worked on that house night and day and eventually sold it for a good profit. They then bought a piece of land and begged and borrowed materials, advice and help from whoever would give it. They designed and built a house in which disabled and able people could live together in comfort. A major magazine ran regular features as the property progressed. After three years they sold it and ploughed the money straight into their dream.

My friend died suddenly a few months ago but not before thousands of kids had holidayed on the farm he made for them, not before they had fed the chickens, milked the goats and occasionally fallen out of their wheelchairs on the adventure course. And not before the government appointed him as an advisor on housing and programmes for disabled people, and not before he saw – and caught – his dream.

It's true that there were lots of disappointments and failures along the way. But learning to live with failure is part of the stock-in-trade of the dreamer. A business consultant once told me, 'It takes fifteen years to become an overnight success.' I have a lot of sympathy with that and I've no doubt that many of those fifteen years are filled with apparent failure. I say 'apparent' because if we don't let failure crush us, there is no more effective mentor.

Theodore Roosevelt put it like this:

It is not the critic who counts, not the man who points out where the strong man stumbled, or where the doer of deeds could have done better. The credit belongs to the man who is actually in the arena; whose face is marred by dust and sweat and blood; who strives valiantly; who errs and comes up short again and again; who knows the great enthusiasms, the great devotions and spends himself in a worthy cause; who at the best, knows in the end the triumph of high achievement, and who, at worst, if he fails, at least fails while daring greatly; so that his place shall never be with those cold and timid souls who know neither victory or defeat. [10]

These days I tread a little more lightly around people's dreams. Dreamers are dangerous people. They break the rules, they frustrate you with their sheer doggedness; but the world is duller without them. Those of us who meet them would do well to have a little humility in their presence, because although they will sometimes fail, they will fail reaching, stretching and, once in a while, they will bring that dream in.

Those who say it can't be done shouldn't get in the way of those who are doing it.

Don't just dream – plant a seed

Though I do not believe that a plant will spring up where no seed has been, I have great faith in a seed. Convince me that you have a seed there and I am prepared to expect wonders.

IIenry David Thoreau,
The Succession of Forest Trees

I was recently a guest speaker at a residential conference for business leaders. I sat in on the last session where one of the other speakers was bringing what had been an incredibly challenging time together to a close. He said, 'Over the past twenty-four hours we have listened to gifted men and women and been motivated to make a difference in our companies and our personal lives but what we have now is a handful of seeds – unless we plant them, they'll never grow.' He was right. Personally I'd sit in a seminar all day just for one good idea. The problem for so many of us is that we can leave the venue with a conference notebook filled with ideas, but, in our hearts, we know they'll never come to fruition, because once we leave the seminar and return to the pressure of normal life we'll never get around to them.

He then produced a table on which were dozens of tiny clay pots. Next to the table was a bag of earth, and in his hand a cluster of seeds. He then asked every delegate right there and then to come forward, take a pot and some earth and plant a seed. He said if you want to see a vision grow there are three conditions: first you have to have a seed, then you need to actually plant it and, third, it helps if you remember to water it occasionally!

One by one the delegates came forward and planted a seed. (If they remembered the third injunction and watered it a little then, by now, they have a full-grown plant.) But one man held back. It's true that he collected his pot, and I saw him scoop a little earth into it. I was there as the speaker handed him a seed. But he slipped it into his pocket. Perhaps he didn't want to get his hands dirty; maybe he felt the exercise beneath him. But more likely he thought, 'I'll do it later.' Forty people walked out of that room having just planted a dream – and one man left with the dream in his pocket.

Over the past twenty-five years I have met countless men and women of vision. These people have dreams for their careers, their departments and their businesses. To be in the company of these characters is exciting – they are going to change the world! And yet so few visions ever get a chance to fail, let alone succeed.

There are some words that are immediately recognisable in every language: you can yell 'taxi' in JFK airport in New York, on Entebbe Street in Uganda, and in Red Square, Moscow; you may not be able to speak Spanish, Chinese or Italian but say 'hotel' and somebody in Madrid, Beijing, or Rome will point you in the right direction. Some new words have now been added to that list. They are called 'billion dollar brands'. One of them is 'McDonald's'.

But how did the McDonald's story start? The official account is that it began with a man called Ray Kroc standing outside a hamburger stall in Fresno, California, and dreaming that one day he could sell this product all over the USA. But that's not true – you don't get franchises out of dreams, otherwise we wouldn't be able to move for them. No, it started when Kroc made a phone call. He actually picked up a telephone and asked how much it would cost to purchase some rolls and beef. It started when he … began. A Chinese proverb says, 'Even a journey of a thousand miles begins with a single step.'

It's not true just of the business world. Almost everybody you meet has a dream. I often talk to people who tell me that one day they will write a book, learn a language, get fit or spend more time with their family. Every one of those dreams is real and sincere. And yet few of those dreams will ever be caught – will ever be translated into reality. If dreams are the hope, and beginning is the key, then what stops us from getting started, to giving birth to our visions?

The main reason we give is 'time'. We say, 'If only I had more time …' or 'When I retire I'm going to learn to paint,' or 'When I get promotion I'll have more time for you and the kids.' The fascinating thing is we discover that when we suddenly have 'more time', it is quickly taken up. For years we've been promised an assistant – this man or woman who will take all the paperwork off us so we can get back to doing what made our company successful in the beginning. And suddenly that person arrives. Do we now have the time to see our visions fulfilled? Hardly. The 'new' time we have is somehow eaten up. It's hard to put our finger on it – it's just that life is still so busy. We wonder how we ever managed before.

And so we become consumed with the pursuit of finding 'time-saving devices.' Did your great-grandmother have a dishwasher, a freezer the size of a small mortuary, e-mail or any of the myriad of 'time-saving' devices that you possess? And how are they working? Do you have more time than she did? In our home we spend most of our time taking our 'time-saving' devices to be repaired, or working to pay the premiums on the insurance policies to keep them humming. The other day somebody tried to sell us a carpet-sweeper so we didn't have to get the vacuum cleaner out every day. We almost bought it until we realised we had bought the vacuum so that we didn't have to get the sweeper out every day.

I rarely meet people who tell me they have plenty of time on their hands. Whether it's a company director, a single parent, a baker, student or nurse, people use phrases like, 'I'm rushed off my feet', or 'There just aren't enough hours in the day.' Well, let's think about that. Every day has exactly the same number of minutes – 1,440. How many would you like? Imagine I could wave a wand and give you an extra twenty – or sixty – how many would be enough to mean you weren't under pressure?

I am sometimes asked to run courses on time management – but I refuse to run a conventional one because I know that even if I could 'create' an extra hour a day for those busy executives, it wouldn't help in the long run. They would just fill it with more of the same old frenetic activity. And I refuse to talk about 'saving time' because you can't save time – you can only spend it. When people say, 'I've saved an hour', I ask them to produce it. No, if we are to catch our dreams we somehow have to learn to do that within the limited time we have. The truth is that everybody wants more time but everybody has all the time there is. It is the one thing that the poorest beggar on the streets of Calcutta and the most powerful person in the world has exactly the same amount of. Every man, woman and child begins each new day with a bag filled with 1,440 minutes. The problem is the thief of time.

Shortly after Dianne and I were married our home was burgled. Whoever broke in on that night in June was considerate to say the least: they didn't trash the place, they didn't take very much, and they didn't even wake us. In fact it took a while to dawn on us that somebody had stolen some of our few possessions. At breakfast I said to Dianne, 'What's the time?' She replied, 'There's a clock on the dresser.' But there wasn't. And neither was there a radio on the table near the door nor a pair of brass candlesticks on the sideboard. Without our knowing, and from literally under our noses, the thief had quietly dispossessed us.

On the stroke of midnight, when that bag full of the minutes of a new day is delivered to our bedside, the thief of time begins to operate. This malevolent creature will rob us of time with our family, of the chance to get promotion or pass an examination.

His name is 'Later' and he has dedicated his life to stealing people's time and vision. Whenever he meets somebody who has hopes, ambitions, ideas, dreams, he says, 'Very good. But not today. Today you should clean the car, get your teeth checked, or make that "ring Clive" phone call that's been on your desk for six months.'

And as you wake he will be at your bedside to encourage you to apply for the job, to deal with the debt problem that is crushing you, to make the phone call that could transform your business, or begin to mend a broken relationship in your family, but he will urge you to some other task first. He will guide you to catch your dream – later.

There is no hope of you and me seeing our dreams realised unless we deal with this creature. His power lies in his stealth; if you see him, you have him beaten. If you would be a dream-catcher begin *today*. No matter how small the step towards your goal – start it. If the task seems too great then break it down and begin a small part of it.

I remember when I attempted to write my first book. The publisher told me he wanted it to contain

65,000 words. I said, 'I don't think I know 65,000 words!' For weeks I stared at the contract to write the book and promptly did something else. I found myself tackling jobs I had managed to ignore for years. Somehow they suddenly became pressing. I sorted the books on my shelves and cleaned out the drawers in my desk. And then one day I realised it was the thief of time urging me to postpone the task of writing the first page. At the very moment of recognising him, he lost his power over me and I decided to *begin*. I sat at the desk, ignored the phone that had just started to ring, and wrote ten chapter headings – just that – ten lines on a sheet of A4 paper. The next day I wrote the first two pages of chapter one.

When the publishers sent me a copy of *Loving Against the Odds* I held it in my hand. I had written a book. It was a dream, and by God's grace I had caught it. Since that day my books have sold in over ten languages worldwide. Almost every week somebody writes to me to say that one of those books has changed their lives. It all began with *Loving Against the Odds*. But to write that book involved me in a daily battle with 'Later'. And he very nearly robbed me of it. In fact he almost had me trade that book for a tidy office.

Remember that dreams are contagious

Companies need dreamers for the simple reason that such people do not only bring their own dreams in – they envision others. When he was a young man Roger Bannister had a dream – it was to be the first human being in history to run a mile in under four minutes. So many people told him it was impossible. Some in the medical profession warned him that the human body was simply not designed to run that fast. In fact they did some tests and showed him that they had discovered that if a human being tried to do it, the heart would explode within the chest cavity.

On a dark and overcast day in May 1954 Roger Bannister broke the tape in 3 minutes 59.4 seconds. Not only was his heart still in place but he seemed to have affected a few other hearts for, by the end of

1957, sixteen other people had broken the four-minute mile. That's why companies need dreamers.

When Helen Keller was nineteen months old she contracted an illness that left her blind, deaf and dumb. When she was six years old Helen began learning to speak by pressing her fingers on her tutor's larynx to 'hear' the vibrations. She learned to read and write in Braille and eventually graduated from Radcliffe College, Cambridge, Massachusetts. She founded the Helen Keller Home for Blind Children and toured the world lecturing. She was once asked, 'Can you think of anything worse than being blind?' She said, *'Yes. To be able to see and have no vision.'*

You have a right to dreams

Some of us believe we have no right to dreams. The world is full of people who have been told all their lives that they are useless. The words of others have become a self-fulfilling prophecy and they seem to fail at anything to which they turn their hand. But to be a dream-catcher we must believe that when God created us he didn't make a mistake.

We may not be the shape we want to be, or have the looks we would choose; we may carry scars from a broken home or an abusive father; we may have a disability, but we still have a right to dreams. Some of us have been told so often that we are useless we have come to believe it. But it's not true.

When I was a child I remember only three books in our home: a Bible, the *Shorter Oxford English Dictionary*, and an atlas. Dad was a postman; my mother cleaned offices to help make ends meet. I'm not sure how it happened but I passed the eleven-plus examination for the local grammar school. The second I arrived there I felt I didn't belong. The kids that I now mixed with had cars, and houses with bathrooms; their parents were able to help them with their homework or pay to have tutors and, as I learned on a visit to a friend, they used toilet paper instead of the local newspaper cut into squares.

I did poorly at school. I well remember at the end of my first year the teacher reading the examination results in descending order. There were thirty-four children in our class and as our form-teacher's voice droned on through the twenties I can remember the looks on some of those children's faces. They were looks not of shame or fear, but sheer despair. They were the looks of those who believed they were losers. On one occasion I came last: the worst child, the stupidest pupil, the boy who would fail.

My life changed the day I met a dream-catcher. I was sixteen years old and he was in his mid-thirties. His name was Arthur. He and his wife could not have children of their own but they were our youth club leaders and in truth they had hundreds of kids. They lived in two rooms of the terraced house that they shared with Arthur's mother. All kinds of kids came under the influence of those special people – kids who were sporting, and those who nobody wanted in their team; kids who had stable homes, and those who weren't sure if their father was ever coming back; kids who attended the little church at which the club was held, and those who threw stones at its windows. But whoever you were, and whatever your background, and no matter how much hassle you caused him, Arthur had a secret strategy. He made you feel special. He told us that God loved us just as we were, and that he and Margaret believed in us. No matter what friends or teachers thought of you, when you entered Arthur's house you felt like a king.

One day he said to me, 'Rob, I think you may have a gift of public speaking.'

'No way!' I said. 'I've never done any of that stuff.'

But he persevered. He had me giving speeches to a mirror on the wall; to Margaret as she made the tea; and then, one day, to twenty or so kids from another youth club. Arthur was one of the worst public speakers I have ever heard but somehow he taught a few of his youth club to do it.

I remember standing in front of audiences when I was seventeen or eighteen years old and thinking, 'I must be dreaming.' The strange thing about dreams is that when they start to come true you wonder whether there are any more out there.

Some years later I was a joint senior partner in a large provincial legal practice, had co-founded one of the most successful legal consultancies in the United Kingdom, was lecturing to lawyers across the world, and had been a keynote speaker at international law conferences. One night I was in Vienna about to address a thousand leaders at an international business conference. I rang Arthur from the hotel and said, 'You taught me to do this. Thank you.' Last year I was in the USA promoting one of my books and the radio station got him on line without telling me. There I was in a radio studio in Colorado Springs when suddenly Arthur's voice came through the speakers. They told me later they requested him to 'do it live' but he had been practising all week! They asked him what he thought of the boy who went to his youth club. He said that he was proud. I cried on air.

Did I have dreams as a child? Of course I did. Do we not think that kids hanging around the corner shop in the middle of an inner city have dreams? Do I not believe that the young offenders I visit in prison who sit hour after hour in a room six feet by ten have dreams? But the truth is that dreams are not enough. We need help to fulfil them. More than that, we have a responsibility as individuals and companies to help each other catch our dreams. I have no doubt there are tens of thousands of kids who have been written off as drop-outs, failures, or even criminals, who more than anything else need to meet an 'Arthur' – a dream-catcher.

You have a right to dreams too. Individuals have the right to dream of what might be, companies need to recapture a vision they may have lost. Try to find somebody who will help you catch those dreams; be prepared for some failures, but most important of all take a step today – no matter how small – towards catching that dream – actually begin. *Plant that seed!*

When I was ten years old I met Trevor Porter who was on his way home from a date with Carol Perkins – that's Carol Perkins from the corner of my street; the unassailable Carol Perkins; the Carol Perkins whom I had thought didn't even look at boys unless they looked like Elvis and rode a Harley Davidson. And this was Trevor the class clown; Trevor who didn't own a pogo stick let alone a motorbike; Trevor who'd never had a date with *anybody*.

'Trevor', I said with my mouth wide open, 'how *did* you do it?'

'Oh,' he said. 'I really like her. So I asked her.'

He *asked* her.

EXECUTIVE BRIEFING

For individuals

❑ The following are some 'thieves of time' that can stop us even beginning to fulfil our dreams. Which are most likely to steal *your* time?

- I put off making decisions.
- I don't establish my priorities.
- I can't say, 'No'.
- I am often interrupted.
- I find it hard to delegate.
- I rarely have time to plan.
- I love meetings.

❑ Is your life being hampered by the unfulfilled dreams of the past? You may have to dig back a little in your personal history to answer this. Are those dreams still viable? If not, give that dream a clean burial now. This doesn't mean there are no dreams left for you, rather that you stop believing that 'my life is ruined for ever because my father made me become a doctor when my heart was in acting'.

❏ If seeing your dream fulfilled could begin with something small, what stops you planting a seed today? If the dream is a long journey, is there a first step you could take today? Not a hope, or a promise, but an actual step – making a phone call, booking a course, *taking a decision*.

❏ Is it the fear of failure that stops you at least beginning to see your dream realised? It's true that once you do begin you will be exposed to the possibility of failure, but at least you will have *begun*. In his inaugural address on 4 March 1933, Franklin D. Roosevelt said, 'The only thing we have to fear is fear itself.'

❏ Can you think of any person who might be a 'dream-catcher' to you? Remember the qualities you are looking for in this person: someone who will bring you down to earth when you are in 'pink flamingo' mode, somebody wiser than you, but above all somebody who believes in you and in your dream.

❏ Is there another person for whom you could be a 'dream-catcher'?

For companies

The problem with most people in business is that they have stopped dreaming.

❑ Is there any possibility that your company has lost the sense of vision that it once had?

❑ Do those who lead have time to catch fresh visions, or has the entrepreneurial spirit been extinguished by the demands of keeping the show on the road?

Those who say it can't be done shouldn't get in the way of those who are doing it.

❑ Does your company suffer from a negative element in the decision-making process that makes it hard to take any concrete action – let alone catch your dreams?

Drop in on a typical partners' meeting. There are five people around the boardroom table. The dream is in place but it needs an initial decision. All they have to do is to decide whether to do black or white.

Senior Partner: 'Well, it's decision time –

let's hear what you think. I think we should go with black.'

Don: 'Black.'

Celia: 'Black.'

Ian: 'Black.'

The senior partner can't believe what's happening – it looks as though after fifteen years they might decide something. In the distance she can see a vision of a dream being realised.

Senior Partner: 'Well, it's just you left, Paul – what do you think?'

Paul: 'Grey ... I mean I can't really decide. There are so many considerations. Could we take this forward to the next meeting? I'll write a paper on it.'

Which is why somebody said, 'Most partners meetings are cul-de-sacs down which good ideas are lured and then quietly strangled.'

❏ Is there any way that employees could be encouraged to have and share 'dreams' for the company?

❏ Is it possible that in some small way the company could help employees fulfil personal dreams?

❏ Do you have a corporate dream?

TUESDAY 6 NOVEMBER, 10.05 P.M.

Tom had already told the young man what the subject was for this week's lesson, and as Jack climbed the hill towards the professor's cottage his heart was heavy. His mind went back almost five weeks to that first evening in the library when he'd met the man he'd mistaken for the janitor and to the reason he was there in the first place. He stopped for a moment at the top of the hill and looked down on the campus. He was trying desperately to understand his father. For a minute he closed his eyes and as he did it was as if he could see him …

David, Jack's father, liked to leave the office last. He had left last for ten years. He had left last whether or not the work demanded that he stay. There was always another thing to do: a client to ring who'd be impressed that you rang him at home at nine-thirty in the evening to discuss his case; some document to draft; some paper to shift. It wasn't hard to leave last; you just had to be dedicated to it.

He pushed his chair back and looked around him.

He loved the place at night. From the window at his right he could look along the embankment of the river and to the left catch the twin towers of the new bank that pierced the skyline. But he always tired quickly of the view outside and his eyes strayed around his office. It was quite simply the best office in the whole block. It was true it wasn't the largest but it was the most impressive. This was his kingdom.

David made his way through the deserted reception and into the street, and, as he did, he spotted a taxi. He barked directions to the cabbie – it was best never to let them decide the route – and reached for his mobile phone. 'I'm on my way – OK? … Well, leave it in the oven – I won't wake you.'

As the cab pulled up he glanced up at his house. In that brief moment before fumbling in his pocket for some change he took it all in: the sweeping drive, the manicured lawns, and then the sheer size of the place. It had been his ambition and he had made it happen. All the lights were out.

He asked the driver to drop him at the pavement and he began to walk along the gravel drive. At least the sensor on the infra-red welcomed him and he blinked for a moment as the security light hit his eyes. He made no attempt to open the door quietly – it would be nice if he woke somebody and there was some life in the place – but when he entered the hall the house was still dark and quiet. For some reason that he couldn't understand he felt a deep and crushing sadness as he stood there. He glanced at the long antique dresser base filled with photographs: Jack with just two teeth, Suzie when she was a bridesmaid, Jack's graduation, his own wedding.

If you remain still in an old house at night it will speak to you. In the middle of the creaks and sighs of old timber, it will release its memories. David had never been still, he had never for a moment stopped to think. But just now he stood and closed his eyes as the house took him back down the years.

In his mind's eye he saw a small boy – not quite nine years old – running towards him. 'Dad! Dad! I'm in the team. I'm in the team!'

He saw himself the next day on the touchline with the other fathers standing in the pouring rain, all suddenly professional managers and all yelling inane advice, and thinking that if only the others passed more to their boy the team would be in front. He heard the final whistle, saw the look of sheer joy on Jack's face that he had got the winner two minutes from the end, and watched as he ran on to the pitch, put his arm around his son's shoulder and said, 'You were brilliant, Jack. You were like Maradona.' They laughed together as they helped carry the posts back to the dressing-rooms. He saw it all; saw it in colour, in detail, as he stood there in the hall of his home.

But it was *just* in his mind; he had *never* been there. He remembered the reality all too well – recalled getting home late and Mary being silent and himself suddenly saying, 'Well, come on – out with it. What have I done?'

'You forgot, David. That's what you did. You forgot his game again. You'd better go up to him – he's in his room.'

If nothing else David was a brilliant negotiator, and it hadn't taken him long – with the promise of the bike, and the solemn pledge not to miss the next match – to bring a smile to his son's face. And he remembered bringing Jack downstairs laughing, and looking at Mary as if to say, 'See – it was no big deal. He's fine.'

And he remembered so many of those times.

Jack blinked against the tears and suddenly he was at Tom's door. The old man didn't say a thing, just made the coffee, stoked the fire, and lit his pipe. They didn't discuss much that night; Tom just wrote the law down next to the other four and let it be ...

LAW NUMBER FIVE

PUT YOUR FAMILY BEFORE YOUR CAREER

PUT YOUR FAMILY
BEFORE YOUR CAREER

S ome years ago I wrote a book called *The Sixty Minute Father*. Much of it was based on things I believed I'd got wrong when my children were small but, thankfully, young enough for me to have time to change. It was a book written to urge men in their pursuit of 'success' not to miss out on their children's lives. I sent the manuscript to several eminent business leaders and held my breath as to whether anyone would bother to reply. Sir John Harvey-Jones was the first. This is part of what he said:

> *Few people who have led successful lives have also achieved the most important success of all, namely of being a good father and taking part in the joys and extra dimensions that a close relationship with one's family can give.*

The second came from Sir Tom Farmer, Chairman and Chief Executive of Kwik Fit Holdings. Again here is part of what he said:

> *Too often those of us heavily involved in the business world are in danger of losing out on our most important asset – our family.*

I was grateful beyond measure for the generosity of time and spirit that made these busy men make the time and effort to support my book. And grateful also that in so few words they had managed to catch the heart of what I was trying to say – that so many of those whom others consider 'successful' feel they have missed out on the most important area of their lives. Put another way, how can we, who so well understand the value of assets, call ourselves successful if we have, as Tom Farmer put it, '… lost out on our most important asset'?

I am convinced that few of us do it knowingly. My mind goes back to the time when my children were small. I was busy helping to build a business. There was nothing wrong with that, it was simply that I let it become all-consuming. I remember times when they would say to me, 'Dad, will you listen to me read this?' and I would say, 'Sure I will, but could we do it later?' I meant 'later', I didn't mean 'never'. How was I to know that the day would come when they would stop asking? Why didn't somebody tell me that the 'slower day' I was promising myself, when I would have more time for the things that mattered most to me, was never coming?

I wasn't stupid. I could probably have understood. So why did nobody point out to me the sheer futility of working so hard to give my kids what I didn't have as a child, that I didn't have time to give them what I *did* have? And was there nobody around who could warn me that the door of childhood shuts so quickly and so finally?

In those days there was no escaping the phone in our home. It would ring during meals and halfway through bedtime stories. Many of those calls were to do with business. The caller usually began by saying, 'I'm sorry – I never ring people at home' which made it hard to work out who it was on the other end of my phone line. The next thing the caller invariably said was, 'This will only take a minute.' If anybody says that to you they're lying – it will take at least ten minutes. And worse than that, by the time you go back to what you were doing, the child who was listening to the bedtime story is asleep – and your dinner's in the dog.

But now I have the benefit of hindsight. I am twenty years down the road and I have helped build that business. I have been privileged to have been invited into many companies as a consultant, written seven books and lectured all over the world. All those have involved me in receiving thousands of business calls, many of which the caller has described as 'urgent'. The strange thing is I can't remember one – not *one* – that couldn't have waited ten minutes while I finished a bedtime story.

I remember somebody saying to me around that time, 'What's the secret of your success?' I mumbled some trite answer about hard work and being in the right place at the right time. But if Tom Farmer was right, and I was in danger of losing my most important asset, the question was a cruel joke. How can somebody who has lost their greatest asset be successful?

Since those days I have met many 'successful' men and women and it seems to me that we use the wrong word in describing them. We should not talk of 'success' but rather ask, 'What is the secret of your *achievement*?' Many of these people have little peace in their lives. Their bodies are cracking up, they have frequent headaches, get ill on holiday and find an increasing irritability in dealing with others. They don't sleep well and tranquillisers have become a way of life. They have little time for family. Put like this, the answer to the question, 'What is the secret of your achievement?' may be: 'I have achieved these things at the cost of my health and by putting the things that matter most to me on the back burner for twenty years or so. That's how I've done it.'

We live in a society that so often measures our success by what we own, the kind of house we live in, the car we drive and where we can afford to go on holiday. But we would do well not just to ask the price of these things, but the cost – how much extra time we have to work to pay for them.

A Canadian businessman tells me he has to work

long hours and couldn't entertain doing a job that paid less, but allowed him a less frantic lifestyle, because he has so many financial commitments. One of those commitments is a cabin in the woods for weekends. I asked him if he got much use out of it. He said, 'Well, not a lot, to be honest. The cabin is a three-hour drive away. I try to leave work early on a Friday but by the time I've fought the Vancouver traffic we don't get there until 10 p.m. On Saturdays there are usually jobs that need to be done there and so I drive to the nearby town to get DIY supplies. We normally leave early on Sunday afternoon so that we miss the heavy traffic on the drive home.' He should keep his cabin. If the real cost of owning it ever hits him, he'll need it so he can have somewhere to scream without anybody hearing.

About five years ago a very wealthy banker asked to meet me in the Dorchester Hotel, London. Our appointment was set for five o'clock in the afternoon. By five-thirty there was no sign of him but a member of the hotel staff approached me, gave my host's apologies for being a little late, and invited me to order tea and cakes on his account. I glanced at the menu; the cakes cost more than the average semi-detached. I chose four. Twenty minutes passed and I was invited to order more cakes. I politely refused.

At ten to six, red-faced and bursting with regret, my appointment arrived. His opening line was, 'I've been involved in a really big take-over in the City – forgive me. Now, would you like some cakes?'

I was truly caked-out. 'No,' I said, 'they've looked after me very well. But I'm sorry, I'm already a little late for my next appointment. We'll have to reschedule.'

'Well, at least let's have *some* time together,' he said. 'I've got a car outside – I'll take you.'

He did, indeed, have a car outside. In fact, his limousine took up most of the outside. We sank into the leather of the rear seats and as I looked around, desperately hoping that somebody I knew would come along, he gave instructions to the chauffeur.

He seemed agitated. I sensed a man who had little peace in his life. His mind must still have been on the deal because he suddenly turned to me and said, 'Many of those youngsters back there in the City are never going to make it.'

'My fear', I replied, 'is for those who *do*.'

He turned to face me, 'Whatever do you mean?'

'Well', I said, 'even if your goal is to accumulate as much money as possible, you still have to have enough time to spend the stuff.'

'You try telling that to the people I work with back there,' he retorted.

'I'll tell you when they'll believe me,' I replied. 'When they're sixty-five years old, and at the very top of the pile. And suddenly they will look around and ask themselves, "Is this all there is? Is this what I have given forty years of my life for?" They've missed their kids growing up, they have no real friends to speak of, and their body is shot. Then they'll believe me.'

The car arrived at my next appointment and I shook the banker's hand as I left. As I stepped into the street, I looked back; he seemed sad. The door slammed, the car pulled away and then suddenly he wound down the window and yelled, 'Could we meet again?'

'Sure,' I shouted back. 'Give me a ring.'

I watched as the limo fought its way into the traffic in Kensington High Street, watched it as it bore him to the next deal, saw the shoppers turn to wonder who was behind the tinted glass, saw the envy in some of their eyes, and then it was gone, lost in the London traffic. I never saw him again.

As I think of him now my mind goes back to another man, a successful man, a powerful man, but somebody who had found little time for family or friends. He had devoted everything to his career. But it had its compensations. When he strode along the corridor to his office, the one in the corner of the building overlooking the lake, the junior executives practically bowed. This man was like a feudal baron. The filing cabinets contained his conquests and if he left his office door ajar he could see his minions rushing to fulfil his every whim.

Who would have thought that something as simple as a birthday could have robbed him of all this? But it did. I was there when it happened. He reached sixty years of age. And suddenly he was surrounded by 200 of his staff and his deputy said, 'Bill, we're going to miss you. You have been the inspiration behind this company for over twenty years ...' As the speech droned on Bill glanced to his left and saw that his nameplate had already been taken from his door and a new one lay on a nearby table. '... And so, Bill, we'd like to give you a little gift.' Somebody pressed it into his hands. Ironic that it was a clock.

The few who stayed to the end of the party said that Bill was the last to leave. He took one last look around the office, turned off the lights himself and walked into the street. It was dark and raining hard; he turned the collar of his coat up, pressed the clock to his chest, and he was gone.

But it wasn't the end of the story. For the following three months you could sometimes see Bill, dressed for work, walking up and down the patch in front of his old office, hoping to meet somebody who would remember him for who he used to be.

I meet men and women every day – successful men

and women – who have often achieved beyond their wildest dreams. These are men and women whom others would love to emulate and yet they would give all they possess if only they could change the past. So what is their great regret? Is it that they could have been more effective salespeople, received wider acclaim for their academic papers, or pushed harder to get that promotion? Rarely. No – the regret is almost always in the area of relationships.

Some years ago I was asked to speak to a large financial institution on the matter of balancing home and work. The senior executives and sales force had all been gathered for a day in which they had examined the performance for the previous year and set goals for a new millennium. I was the closing speaker. I commended them for the success they had known and acknowledged that, to achieve it, somebody somewhere had worked long hours and made many sacrifices.

But then I urged those successful men and women not to forget the fact that although work is important, when they are older it is in the area of relationships that they will crave success. I warned them that, if they had children, those kids would be grown and gone before they knew it. As I spoke I saw the usual looks of disbelief from the young and knowing nods from those with a few grey hairs. And then I said, 'The days when your children want you to watch them in school plays, teach them to fly a kite, and listen to that story over and over again are very limited. The time is hurtling towards you when you're going to say to a fourteen-year-old, "Do you fancy going fishing this weekend?" and he'll reply, "Do you mind if we don't, Dad – I said I'd go out with some friends."'

I told them of a little maths I did one day that changed my life. I worked out the number of days in the first eighteen years of my children's lives – 6,575. No amount of success, money or prestige can buy us one day more. If your child is ten years old, you have 2,922 left. I said, 'I understand as well as anybody the pressures of modern business life, but those days of your children's lives are irreplaceable: so far as is possible, try not to miss one of them.'

When I finished, the chairman, a man of about

sixty, stood up to thank me. He was obviously having some difficulty speaking, but somehow he concluded his remarks and took his seat next to me on the podium. And then I saw that his eyes were full of tears. As unobtrusively as I could, bearing in mind that we were in full view of the audience, I asked him if he was all right. He turned towards me and said, 'I'm OK. I just found it all very moving. I've been overseas for five days and when I got back I said to my fourteen-year-old boy, "Well, have you missed me?" He said, "No, Dad – because you're never here."' He went on, 'You know what really upset me? It was that my son wasn't being sarcastic. He was just articulating what has become for us a *lifestyle*.'

I reached out and touched his arm and said, 'It's never too late.' I was well-intentioned but I wasn't being completely honest. The truth is that although that man may still build a wonderful relationship with his son, nothing could give either of them back the years that were gone. At the time, the chance to stand on the touchline of football matches seemed as though it would be there forever, and when that father said, 'Next week, son – I'll be there then,' he meant it. It was just that there were always business plans to write and accountants to listen to; there were hundreds of people who had demanded a piece of him. But his son hadn't demanded; he had just *asked* – until one day he had just stopped asking.

Why would we live like that? What amount of money or power would lure us into an existence where we have an incredible standard of living but such a low quality of life? The answer is unpalatable. What drives us is the illusion of *the race*. To understand the illusion we must first understand the reality. Reality is the Olympic marathon runner, getting up at five in the morning to endure darkness and cold as he pounds the roads in training. It is the forsaking of time with family, or friends, or entertainment, because for the immediate future the race must be all. It is the dedication of oneself to a dream – to the possibility of the prize. And as he runs the streets he dreams of the moment when he ascends the winner's rostrum and holds his medal high as his country's anthem is played.

Now imagine the unthinkable. Imagine that the

training was for forty years. Forty years of sacrifice, forty years of dedication to the goal. But at the very last moment an official comes and says, 'There is no prize. There is no medal. The winner's rostrum was an illusion.'

And is it possible to build strong successful companies without the trick – without the promise of the prize one day – the prize that is always a little further away? And is it possible to carve a career and still be a human *being*, not just a human *doing*? Yes, it is, but only if we say the unthinkable – that tomorrow does not hold the prize – only today. Nothing else will keep us from the foolishness of saying, 'One day I'll have more time', or 'My retirement package will be wonderful.' More and more young people are rejecting what they perceive to be the futility of doing it all for tomorrow. They are saying, 'We want to work for companies that allow us to live *today*.' Are they less gifted, less committed or unwilling to work long hours if needed? No. They are simply saying, 'Don't sell me this as a forty-year lifestyle with the promise that one day it will all be worthwhile.'

The 'Quality of Working Life' report by the Institute of Management showed that an increasing number of younger executives are finding excessively long hours unacceptable.[11] The *Financial Times* commenting on the study said, 'This younger generation may yet start believing in the long-hours culture. But if it does not succumb, it could be the force behind the change.'[12]

The professional magazine, *Accountancy Age*, reports that female entrepreneurs can feel they are not taken seriously if they tell clients that they have to leave to pick up their children. Often they have to pretend they have a meeting at 3.30 p.m. 'We have to feel confident enough about ourselves,' says a self-employed tax consultant. 'I don't believe having another commitment makes me a second-class person. A macho working culture that demands longer hours despite home commitments can exacerbate this problem.'[13]

A recent survey of more than a hundred partners, assistant solicitors and HR managers of the top 40 legal firms in the UK showed that forty per cent of female assistant solicitors would reject an offer of partnership, citing stress and long hours as the reason. Some eighty-six per cent of women partners said they were unhappy with the career paths available, and there was strong support for alternative structures. Flexible arrangements or formalising flexible working were the most popular alternatives being considered by HR managers. Anthea Grainger, Chairwoman of the Association of Women Solicitors, said that the dissatisfaction with career paths 'will make firms realise they have to adjust their practices if they want to keep their workforces'. [14] In another survey, only just over half of the respondents agreed that their firm 'gives me the chance to lead a full life outside work'. [15]

I believe we are seeing the emergence of a new style of leader. These men and women see clearly that the sharpest and most creative people need to have lives outside the office. Even more than that, they themselves want to occasionally kick the leaves. In short they are saying, 'Give me a little time now, let me enjoy the prize as I go – and when I'm sixty you can keep the clock.'

When I was halfway through writing this book a

friend of mine attended a seminar given by Kevin Kaiser. Kaiser had been Assistant Professor of Finance at INSEAD, the international business school based in France, and, in addition to several MBA and PhD courses, he had conducted seminars for international firms and investment banks across Europe. My friend said that Kaiser was brilliant – here was one of the brightest minds in the financial world sharing what he believed were trends, pitfalls and opportunities.

But it wasn't Kaiser's financial modelling that impressed my colleague. It was a simple story he told of his own life. I was determined to speak with him and tracked him down in Paris where he is Vice-President of Product Development in bfinance.com, a company responsible for creating the leading web-based community for financial executives in Europe. He told me his story.

When he was a professor at INSEAD and married with two children, Kaiser took a post as visiting professor at Northwestern University in Chicago. One day he got an e-mail. It told him that, in essence, his marriage was over. His world fell apart, but life was about to get even more complicated. The investment bankers, Goldman Sachs, asked him to join them. The partner who headhunted him said, 'Kevin, you've got what it takes to be a great investment banker. And there is no better lifestyle than at Goldman Sachs.' The offer they made him was practically irresistible. Within four weeks Morgan Stanley, Goldman's competitors, had matched it. The race to get Kaiser was on.

He turned both down and said he wanted to get back to Paris to see if it was possible to save his marriage. It seemed that it wasn't.

Kaiser decided it was time to try to make a new start and resolved that he would take one of the jobs with the investment banks. And it was at the moment when he was trying hard to decide whether to take what he called 'an obscene amount of money' from either one or the other that international consultants, McKinsey and Co., came on the scene. They did so via one of their top people, Tim Koller, who co-authored *Valuations*. He asked Kevin to meet with him to consider joining them.

Kaiser wasn't interested. It wasn't that he didn't

respect McKinsey and Co – he had taught hundreds of their consultants and he knew what they stood for – but if he was to move from academia to the world of business he thought, why do it for half the money the investment banks were paying? He said no. Five times. Eventually he realised he would be in Amsterdam teaching at the same time as Koller would be there and he rang him and offered to meet him on a Wednesday evening.

By now Kaiser was getting used to the attention paid him by some of the most interesting companies in the financial world, which made it all the more difficult for him to understand what happened next. Koller said he was very sorry but although he desperately wanted to see Kaiser, he couldn't meet that evening as the following day he was flying out of the country and it would be the last chance for a while to have dinner with his wife and kids – and he'd promised them not to miss it.

Kaiser said, 'I was literally astounded. In many companies you'd have been fired for admitting thinking it, let alone saying it.' He went on, 'I knew then that I wanted to meet these people.' They met for breakfast on the Thursday morning.

And it was over croissants and coffee in the Amsterdam Ambassador Hotel that one of the most unusual deals in the financial/consultancy world was done. McKinsey and Co. were offering to pay him only half the salary of the investment banks, yet Kaiser agreed to join them. But there was a very unusual condition. Kaiser only had access to his two children every other weekend and he said to Koller, 'For those weekends, wherever I am in the world you must fly me home so I am in Paris by 4 p.m. on Friday and leave me alone – no phone calls – no hassle – until 8 p.m. on Sunday night. I'll work twenty-four hours a day for you for the rest of the time – I'll be so busy I won't have time to eat – but you must give me that protected time with my children. It matters to me.' Koller agreed.

It took just under a month for the documents to be ready to sign and before the ink was on the paper the Goldman Sachs partner asked to meet Kaiser again. He tried time and again to get him to change his mind. At one stage Kaiser said, 'OK. I'll join you. But it has to be the same deal. Every other weekend I'm at home with my kids and for that brief period – untouchable.'

The partner said, 'Kevin, you know I can't do that. You're making a big mistake.'

For the two and half years Kaiser was with McKinsey and Co. he was home every other weekend and his phone was still until 8 p.m. on the Sunday evening.

I understand it's an unusual situation but I found it a fascinating story. The characters are compelling. The large investment bank, the young professor, the international consultants. But, at its heart, a man who said to himself: I have such a limited time when I can see my kids – just two weekends a month – and if my success can't even buy me some quality time with them, then no amount of money you can pay me will compensate for that. I refuse to consider myself successful on other terms.

A couple of years ago I was lecturing to 100 or so business men and women. I was in the middle of a session where I was talking about some of the issues

I have mentioned above. Suddenly a man in the middle of the room interrupted me. He shouted out, 'It's true that I earn a lot of money but I'm doing it for my kids.' As he shouted a vivid illustration came to me that I'd heard used before.

I asked him the name and age of his youngest child. He told me that Ben was two years old. I then asked him to imagine a long, steel building girder that was just four inches wide. I said, 'Now we lay it along Park Lane. It's on the ground and quite safe. Ben and I are at one end and you at the other. Would you walk along it towards me for £50?'

He looked a little startled but he said he would.

'Now we lift the girder by helicopter and suspend it over the Horseshoe Falls in Niagara.'

He'd been there but I reminded him that the falls were 176 feet high and that 600,000 gallons of water per second fell over the 2,600 foot brink. 'You're on one side and Ben and I are on the other. It's rainy and windy; in fact the girder is swaying a little. The water is crashing and thundering below us.'

I thought I saw him change colour.

'Now will you walk along the girder to us for £50?'

In no uncertain terms he told me that he wouldn't.

'Will you do it for £1,000?'

'No.'

'A million?'

'No!'

I got him up to ten million. He still refused. Then I said, 'Now imagine that suddenly through the spray you see that Ben has crawled along the girder and is now fifteen feet out and frozen in fear. He is screaming.'

The man didn't hesitate. From the middle of the Hilton Ballroom we heard a managing director in a pin-stripe suit yell out, 'I'm coming!'

I said, 'Don't ever forget this moment. You care for that child more than anything else on the face of the earth. Don't be so busy being "successful" that you miss his life.'

At the end of the seminar he came to me and said simply, 'You switched a light on for me.'

Here's another light:

A US businessman was at the pier of a small coastal Mexican fishing village when a small boat with just one fisherman docked. Inside the boat were several large yellow-fin tuna. The American complimented the Mexican on the quality of his fish and asked how long it took to catch them.

The Mexican replied, 'Only a little while, senor.' The American asked why he didn't stay out longer and catch more fish. The Mexican said that he had enough to supply his family's immediate needs.

The American then asked, 'But what do you do with the rest of your time?'

The fisherman said, 'I play with my children, take siesta with my wife, Maria, stroll into the village each evening where I sip wine and play guitar with my amigos. I have a full and busy life, senor.'

The American smiled, 'I am a Harvard MBA – that's a degree in business studies – I could help you. You should spend more time fishing and with the proceeds buy a bigger boat, with the proceeds from the bigger boat you could buy several boats, eventually you would have a fleet. Then instead of selling your catch to a middleman you would sell directly to the processor eventually opening your own cannery. You would control the product, processing and distribution.

'You would, of course, need to leave this small coastal fishing village and move to Mexico City, then Los Angeles, and eventually New York City where you would run your expanding enterprise.'

The Mexican fisherman asked, 'But, senor, how long will all this take?'

The American replied, 'Fifteen to twenty years.'

'But what then, senor?'

The American laughed, 'That's the best part. When the time is right you sell your stock to the public and become very rich. You would make millions.'

'Millions, senor? But then what?'

'Then you would retire, move to a small coastal fishing village, where you could sleep late, fish a little, play with your kids, take siesta with your wife, Maria, and stroll to the village in the evenings where you could sip wine and play your guitar with your amigos.'

With just the hint of a twinkle in his eye, the fisherman said, 'Senor – are these business degrees hard to get?'

EXECUTIVE BRIEFING

For individuals

Few people who have led successful lives have also achieved the most important success of all – taking part in the joys and extra dimensions that a close relationship with one's family can give.

Sir John Harvey-Jones

If we have children it's not always possible to give them all the time we would like. Here are some simple action points that don't take long but, when used consistently, make a big difference to our relationships.

- ❏ Children love receiving letters; if you have to be away from home drop them a line.

- ❏ Kneel to talk to toddlers and listen with your *eyes*.

- ❏ Whenever possible try not to take phone calls in time you have designated for your children – buy an answerphone – switch off the mobile.

❏ Develop family traditions. These could be as simple as fish and chips every Saturday night. Your children will remember them when they are grown up.

❏ Eat together whenever possible.

❏ If possible take your child to the place where you work. Let her sit in your place. Tell her how you spend your day.

❏ Plan as soon as possible a half-day with your child when you can spend time alone doing ordinary things together.

❏ Tell your children every day that you love them.

❏ Take a large glass bottle. Fill it with marbles. Let every one of them represent the number of Saturdays you have before your kids reach eighteen. Take out one marble every week.

The great illusions

Consider again the illusions that so often rob us of time with those who matter most to us. Is there one of them that affects you particularly?

- ❏ I'm working such long hours so I can give them all more than I had when I was a kid.

- ❏ Life won't always be this busy – a *slower day is coming*.

- ❏ There will always be tomorrow – the door of childhood stays open for ever.

- ❏ The office/business will never survive without me. (A senior partner in one of the largest firms of accountants took me aside after a seminar I had been leading and said, 'If you want to find out how indispensable you are, take a bucket of water, plunge your hand in and take it out quickly. The hole that's left is how much they'll miss you.')

With partner and friends

Create 'safe havens' for your friends or family when you can give them the dignity of actually being present, not just physically but mentally.

- ☐ Switch the phones off for an hour in the evening.

- ☐ Turn the mobile off in the restaurant. Life will go on and the lack of vibrations will stop you looking as though you've been electrocuted.

- ☐ Set an evening when you and your partner or friends can relax together. If necessary put it in your diary as an appointment. Treat that evening with respect.

- ☐ Learn to laugh again – it's a wonderful therapy.

Remember that good listeners don't:

- ☐ Interrupt.

- ☐ Finish sentences for other people.

- ☐ Let anybody see them looking at their watch.

- ☐ Answer the phone if that gives the impression that the call they take is more important than the conversation they're already having.

For companies

☐ Don't ever say, 'We expect our people to leave their home problems at the office door.' You may as well ask them to leave their left leg there.

☐ Consider that because over 50 per cent of absenteeism is stress-related and much of it emanates from family trauma, any resources a company puts into its employees' family life is an investment in a healthier, more committed workforce.

☐ Consider in-house training that includes the issue of work–life balance. Leading edge companies are already doing this.

☐ Consider an in-house library on family-related issues – parenting, relationships, dealing with debt or stress. Many employees find it difficult to find resources because their lives are so busy and they simply aren't sure where to look.

☐ Become known as a 'family friendly' company not just because of policy but because of culture.

☐ Don't ever be threatened by an employee who tells you his or her family is more important than their job. You've found a person with values – now channel them to help them succeed for you and still have a life.

Jack loved to watch as Tom opened the old notebook in which he kept his laws and all the notes that went with them. He smiled as he thought how many CEOs would give half their salary to be doing just what he was doing now.

'Well, Prof – what's on for class today?'

Tom smiled, 'I've no doubt that this is one lesson you've already grasped. It's part of the reason you were happy to give some time to the man you thought was the janitor.

'Jack, you sometimes hear people say, "If you want to get on in life, it's not what you know but who you know." That may be true, although often it gets people into positions for which they are just not suitable. Normally in the long run 'what you know' is safer. In fact I have a different idea for you: If you want to be successful, pay attention to those who others call "nobodies".'

The old man seemed to be enjoying himself; his eyes twinkled as he spoke. 'There is nothing that exposes a shallow character more effectively than when a man or woman suddenly changes their behaviour when they realise that they are in the presence of the managing director, whereas they thought they were dealing with the janitor!

'Jack, if you really want to succeed ...'

LAW NUMBER SIX

KEEP THE COMMON TOUCH

The
Heart of
Success

KEEP THE
COMMON TOUCH

According to a national survey, 'If', by Rudyard Kipling, is the nation's favourite poem. It has in it a wonderful line: 'If you can ... walk with kings – nor lose the common touch ...' There are many people who can 'walk with kings'. They have learned how to adapt their demeanour and conversation so as to impress those they deem important. But the real test of character is whether we can walk with kings and yet still have what Kipling called 'the common touch'. This simply means that we are at home with all kinds of people and, as important, they are at home with us. We give dignity to each and a sense that they are important to us. It means you can walk out of a board meeting and thank the junior in the corridor for the way she got the room ready. People try to pass this off as 'patronising' but I have never met any person in any job at all who objects to being treated with respect and gratitude.

People who can only 'walk with kings' believe they can get good service just by shouting, being difficult or reminding people 'who they are'. But generally people are prepared to go the extra mile for those who value them. When you have the 'common touch' you will have an inherent authority that comes only in part from your job title. The trappings of authority may be necessary, but you will elicit respect not just because of what you *do* but because of the kind of person you *are*.

Betty Boothroyd, the former speaker of the House of Commons, had this touch. The speakership is a daunting task – it drove Horace King to drink, and Selwyn Lloyd to distraction – and yet she fulfilled it while keeping the respect of the whole house. She was the first woman in 700 years to hold the post and became the most recognised woman in British politics after Margaret Thatcher. And yet she said, 'I don't get carried away by all this splendour. I'm north country. Down to earth. My roots are under my fingernails.' A close friend said of her, 'There is a feeling that she is one of us. People who are themselves are always impressive. She never tries to be anything else.'

In contrast, I recently heard of a managing director who would have his chauffeur pick him up from his house every day at seven-thirty. The man had strict instructions: he was not to leave the driver's seat and, after his employer had got in the car, he must drive straight off. He was not to engage in any conversation nor was he even to look at his boss in the rear-view mirror. Things went reasonably well for several months until one morning the MD remembered he'd left some papers on his hall table and got straight back out of the car. The chauffeur heard the rear door slam shut, and drove off – only to discover fifty minutes later that he'd left his boss behind. He was sacked.

What a contrast with the attitude of the late Sir John Laing who founded the famous building company. He would drive his Rolls-Royce to work every day, and on one occasion as he was sweeping up the drive towards his headquarters, he sounded his horn and waved at an employee who was walking to work. The man immediately took off his cap and apologised for being in the way. Apparently Sir John looked bemused. 'Oh, no,' he said. 'I was just wanting to say, "Good morning".'

And having the 'common touch' means that you are open to finding talent in unexpected places – even to finding a surprising Factor X. Some years ago in my legal practice we perceived that the way clients were retaining lawyers was changing. More and more were first telephoning to discuss fees before they considered making an appointment. The problem was that as soon as you quoted a fee, a competitor simply knocked a few pounds off it. Some law practices were saying, 'Come back to us when you've got the very lowest quote and we'll beat it.' But the service they were giving was often poor. We believed we needed to win the business not just on cost but on service; to achieve that we needed to get face-to-face with the client. We had a team of people whose job it was to take those calls and persuade the client it was worth her time actually to make an appointment to see us. The skills required to achieve this had nothing to do with legal knowledge – in fact most of the partners were hopeless at it. The team experienced outstanding success.

One day an enquiry came through but all the team members were already taking calls. It eventually got put through to a young typist called Andrea. She put her work aside for a moment and, apparently without too much effort, persuaded the client to come for an interview. The team was impressed and decided to give Andrea another go – with the same result. Although Andrea was a junior typist she was recognised as having exceptional gifting. She became part of the team.

Shortly afterwards I was acting as a consultant to a law practice from another city. They had asked me how to deal with casual enquiries and convert them into clients. Advertising had just been allowed for solicitors but many law practices were spending a fortune on it while still converting only a few of their prospects into fees. I told them about our 'telephone team'. I said that in many practices the partners took these calls but usually they were dismal at it. I wanted to show them a live example of how we achieved such a high success rate, so I called Andrea and asked her to come to the boardroom and show us how she did it. She said, 'Of course – should I bring my book with me?' I had no idea what Andrea's 'book' was. I said, 'Sure – bring your book.'

I will never forget that young woman of not yet twenty walking into the boardroom and sitting to face four cynical legal partners. She was so unfazed it was scary, and, when she was absolutely sure she had their attention, Andrea showed them her book. She had logged every call that came to her and in the right-hand column noted the result – 'success' or 'failure'. There was call after call with 'success!' marked next to it. This woman had discovered something she could do that almost nobody else in that practice – no matter how many law degrees they possessed – could achieve, and when the phone rang, that was her moment.

As Andrea spoke I watched the partners' cynicism melt. It wasn't hard to see how a client would trust this woman. She told her audience in detail how she did it – from the first 'hello' to how she handled it when the client at first refused to make an appointment. As she spoke I suddenly realised that her delivery had slowed and I smiled as I saw why. As the teenager spoke the lawyers were scribbling furiously, trying to capture every word. They were wise not to miss the moment. They were in the presence of a *Factor X*.

I am convinced that many managers can hardly bother to say 'hello' to some people who work for them, not knowing that, if only they would give those people a little time, they would discover a rich vein of talent that could revolutionise their companies.

The 'common touch' can have some very practical implications. Have you ever been in a meeting where everybody is desperately waiting for the coffee to arrive? Suddenly it comes and the junior puts it in the centre of the table with twelve cups and saucers and a plate of biscuits. And that's where it stays, because, even though half the people in the room would kill for a shot of caffeine, nobody wants to be the one to start serving it. Some years ago I had the privilege of attending board meetings with the chairman of a very successful company. This man could and did walk with kings but he had a rare touch of humility. I noticed when the coffee was delivered that, if there was a moment's hesitation, he would stand, set the cups out and start pouring it. He told me later he'd been practising this for years. He said, 'The coffee often goes cold because a crisis of confidence hits people; either they're scared to interrupt the proceedings or they don't want to demean themselves by doing the ordinary tasks.' He urged me, no matter where I was in the perceived 'hierarchy', to get out of my seat and get the job done. 'If you're the managing director,' he said, 'you can bet your bottom dollar that next time you'll be killed in the rush to pour it, and, if they think you're the bottom of the pile, they were waiting for you to do it anyway.'

Remembering the 'common touch' involves not taking ourselves too seriously, and making a habit of treating people with dignity, whatever their status in the company. When we practise this we discover some rather fascinating benefits. First we will meet people on their way up the ladder. The head of sales will remember how you dealt with her when she was a fresh-faced junior. Perhaps even more compelling is the fact that if ever you are forced to make your way down the ladder it's best not to bump into those you stepped on but are now on their way *up*. In short, you will make fewer enemies, but even more important than that – you will carry people with you as you try to implement your plans and strategies. People will give the benefit of the doubt more easily to those they respect and even simply like. And we should never forget how vital the goodwill of the 'foot soldiers' is to the success of any company.

I have acted as a consultant to many legal practices. Sometimes we would spend several hours with the partners formulating a way forward. The next step involved us gathering all the staff together – lawyers, accounts personnel, para-legals, everybody – and unveiling our strategy. I remember on one occasion my partner and myself bringing up a PowerPoint illustration to reveal our plan for the future of the practice. As we went through the strategy we noticed that the secretaries were smiling. It took us a while to work out why and, when we did, we couldn't help smiling ourselves. Those secretaries were saying, 'Just you try.' They knew where real power lies in a legal office; and they're right. Those who are used to power, and spend their lives at the top of organisations, forget how easily people on the lowest rungs of the ladder can make or break the greatest of their plans.

When I was a student and just eighteen years old, Albert Jenkins and I got a job for a local authority counting the wheels on lorries. They were trying to decide whether or not to build a ring road around their city and wanted to monitor the level of heavy traffic flow. They gave us a chair each, together with a pencil and pad, sat us in the middle of a dual carriageway and told us to get counting. And all would have been well if only they had treated Albert with a little dignity – but they didn't. They treated him poorly – as if he was just a number, dispensable, of no value. And so Albert, in his severely demotivated frame of mind, added wheels to lorries. That local authority spent a fortune on planning appeals, surveyors and compulsory purchase orders, but Albert, with his pencil and paper, frustrated their greatest plans.

A few years ago a large London company invited

outside consultants to evaluate their personnel procedures. They were seeking to be awarded a prestigious 'kite-mark'. The person carrying out the initial evaluation told the partners he would want to speak to some of the staff. They agreed. They believed that whoever he picked was going to paint them in a reasonable light. They had spent the last six months talking to their people, listening to them, and stroking them. All the bases were covered – or they would have been covered had not the first person the evaluator asked to see been one of the office cleaners. The question the evaluator asked of him was penetrating: 'Do they invite you to the office party?' He replied, 'I didn't even know there was an office party!' The managing director personally sent him the invitation the next year.

Sir Kenneth Cork was undoubtedly one of the best-known insolvency and bankruptcy practitioners in the UK; some would argue *the* best known. He was responsible for the Cork Report in 1982, a major review of the law relating to insolvency, bankruptcy, liquidations, and receivership. He became Lord

Mayor of London. Few people had a clearer view of what made companies succeed – and fail – than Sir Kenneth. He made famous the early warning signs to watch out for in an insolvent company. Here are just a few:

- Fountain in the entrance hall;
- Corporate flagpole;
- Recipient of the Queen's award for industry;
- Award for best-presented set of annual accounts;
- Rolls-Royce with personalised number plates.

But what was remarkable about the man was his 'common touch'. He had the ability to treat people of all backgrounds and positions in a company with dignity. He passionately believed that it was often the people who were perceived as being at the bottom of the hierarchy who had the best view of what was going wrong with a company, and he loved to talk to them. He said:

To learn about how things have been going wrong at a company, you must certainly not rely on everything you might hear in the boardroom or at head office. There's always somebody there – often in the accounts department – who has a complete grasp of what's been going wrong. He's not necessarily in charge, and very often isn't. As soon as this invaluable person is located you need to use him and his knowledge as much as you can. [16]

Sir Kenneth Cork believed the reason that many companies fail is a lack of communication on the part of the directors sideways among themselves, and downwards and *upwards* from their staff. He said of companies that had failed:

There was a lack of awareness about life in general, of how things and people operate. They often seemed to live in a closed-circuit world of their own ... It is a myth that someone labelled 'a worker' does not understand what managing a company entails ... I am convinced that five times out of ten the answer to saving a business is communication. Unfortunately some managements cannot communicate with themselves, let alone with the workforce. [17]

Just after the end of the First World War my Uncle William, who had been gassed and severely injured in the trenches in France, was walking home from his work as a quarryman. To get to his home he did what he had done every day before he left for the war – he took a short cut across the squire's field. He didn't know that since he had been in Flanders the old squire had become seriously ill and his son was now looking after things. As William walked through the field, smelling of the quarry and dreaming of supper, he heard a voice yell behind him, 'Hey! You!'

William turned as the voice yelled again, 'What do you think you're doing?'

William looked around to see whether anything else was going on that he had missed, and yelled back, 'Are you talking to me?'

By now the distant figure, who turned out to be the squire's son, was just a few feet away and steaming angry: 'You can't walk across this field.'

'I've been walking across this field for fifteen years – it's an extra mile to walk around.'

'Well, you can't now.'

'Look, I'm tired. I've just got back from the war in France, I've just done ten hours at the quarry – get out of my way.'

'I'll call the police.'

'Hold on. How did your father get this field?'

'His father left it to him.'

'And how did *he* get it?

'His father left it to him.'

Apparently, William took the young squire back seven generations until finally he asked,

'And how did *he* get it?'

'He fought for it.'

It was the answer William had been hoping for and rather wearily he took his knapsack off his shoulder, and began to remove his jacket. 'Then,' he said, 'I'll fight *you* for it.'

He was never troubled again.

I've no doubt that the young squire could walk with kings – he probably knew one or two personally – but his life would be blighted unless he could grasp what his father had learnt over many years and was the heart of what Kipling meant in that incredible poem. The principle affects directors, doctors and politicians, in fact all who deal with people: *When you lose the 'common touch', you lose touch completely.*

EXECUTIVE BRIEFING

For companies

❑ Is there anybody in my organisation or department who could have an 'Andrea factor'? (See page 179.)

❑ Is there a way I could test this that is safe both for the employee and the company?

❑ What strategies do we have in place to make every employee feel a sense of worth?

❑ Consider the following extract from the classic, *How to Win Friends and Influence People*, by Dale Carnegie.

In 1936 there were only two people who were paid a salary of a million dollars a year: Walter Chrysler and Charles Schwab. Why did Andrew Carnegie pay Schwab three thousand dollars a day? Because Schwab is a genius? No. Because he knew more about the manufacture of steel than other people? Nonsense. Charles Schwab told me he had men working for him that knew more about the production of steel than he did.

Schwab says that he was paid this salary largely because of his ability to deal with people. I asked him how he did it. Here is his secret in his own words — words that ought to be cast in eternal bronze and hung in every home and school, office and shop in the land: 'I consider my ability to arouse enthusiasm among the men the greatest asset I possess and the best way to achieve that is by appreciation and encouragement.'[18]

For individuals and companies

❏ How can we create an atmosphere in our homes and offices that fosters encouragement and engenders enthusiasm in those around us?

❏ Why do so many managers find it hard to praise? Perhaps because nobody ever praised them or, more likely, just old-fashioned insecurity.

Carnegie himself believed in praise. In fact he designed his own tombstone which read: 'Here lies one who knew how to get around him men who were cleverer than himself.'

❏ What is the single greatest barrier to achieving this?

Remember: people don't normally leave jobs — they leave supervisors.

TUESDAY **20** NOVEMBER, **10.10** P.M.

Jack thought he could smell both the pipe and the coffee as he walked up the path. Tom always told him to walk straight in; sometimes the door stuck and today he pushed it hard. It was locked. Jack suddenly had a bad feeling. Then he saw a note pinned to the door. His name was on the envelope and he tore it open quickly.

> *Jack, I'm sorry we're going to miss our last session. Last night I had a few chest pains and they're fussing over me and insisted I spend a few nights in hospital just to check me out. I'll make sure to get in touch just as soon as they take all the tubes out.*
>
> *I've enjoyed our times together more than you know. You're young but you've done what most people don't achieve in the whole of a lifetime: you've taken a little time to ask 'What's it all about?' All over the world people are rushing about making calls, struggling to survive board meetings, and trying hard to make the books*

balance. Business plans are being written, shredded and written again; office desks are littered with strategy documents that are out of date before the ink is dry and 'unrepeatable opportunities' that will be repeated next week. Don't ever let it get to you so you become cynical, but you must keep your eyes open. We've talked about a lot of things together – finding time for the things that matter, discovering your greatest strength, and finding a dream-catcher, to name just a few – but the really big lesson is ahead, and perhaps it's better you do this one without me. We have lots of knowledge today, Jack, but we seem so very short on wisdom. It's not enough in life to know what you know, you have to know what you believe. Only that will help you fix a course that will see you safely through to the very heart of success.

Your friend, Tom

*PS The last law: **don't settle for success: make a difference – strive for significance**.*

DON'T SETTLE FOR SUCCESS: MAKE A DIFFERENCE – STRIVE FOR *SIGNIFICANCE*

The
Heart of
Success

DON'T SETTLE FOR SUCCESS:
MAKE A DIFFERENCE –
STRIVE FOR *SIGNIFICANCE*

You and I live in incredible times. We can walk outside our homes on a starry night, gaze up at the moon and whisper under our breath, 'We can put people on that.' Those of us who are a little older can remember the excitement when, in December 1967, Dr Christian Barnard gave a South African wholesale grocer, Louis Washkansky, a new heart. But that operation is commonplace now. It was only 100 years ago that the journey from the United Kingdom to Spain could take over three weeks. Just recently I flew from Malaga to London. As we touched down the pilot apologised for the fact that the journey had taken two and a half hours; we had been delayed for *ten minutes*.

There have been more scientific discoveries in the past thirty years than in the whole of previous history put together.

But, in the midst of all the progress, power and posturing of humankind, there is one statistic that ought at least to slow us down, cause us to pause, and make us ponder: the death rate to date is 100 per cent. And not only is that the case but life is *short*. With all our therapies, drugs, exercise programmes and anti-ageing products, we haven't been able to add many years to the estimate an old Jewish poet gave over 4,000 years ago when he said, 'The length of a man's life is three score years and ten, perhaps a little more by strength.'

Of course a few hardy souls have pushed up the average by doing very much better; like Jeanne Calment. She was the first person with a birth certificate to pass 120 years old. She was quite a lady. She took up fencing at eighty-five, and gave up smoking at 115 because she said it was 'getting to be a habit' and 'I find it hard to light up since I've gone blind.' She could recall the Eiffel Tower being erected, and remembered an 'ugly, bad-tempered, alcohol-reeking' man coming into her father's shop in Arles, France to buy paint: his name was Van Gogh. She was once asked if she had any wrinkles and replied, 'Only one – and I'm sitting on it.'

But Jeanne Calment made a comment that we should all have framed and hung on a wall where we see it every day. When she was 115 years old somebody asked her how she saw the future; she replied, 'Very, very short.' It's no secret that the young don't believe this. When we are in our twenties, life seems like those long summer holidays when we were kids. We knew they weren't exactly eternal but they certainly seemed close to it. And yet even there, as August drew to an end and the first chill of September appeared, the long hazy days seemed to vanish so quickly. It will happen to you. The future is short.

Last year I was invited by a British businessman to join him and a few friends for a short break at his Mediterranean villa. He was an unusual man. He was only just forty and yet had helped create a multimillion-pound empire that encompassed property, publishing and franchising. Not bad for somebody who, twenty years ago, was a market trader.

None of his guests had visited his holiday home before and, when I ran into one of them a few days before we left, he asked me what I thought it would be like. I wasn't sure but having seen our friend's home, office and stables, I said, 'Don't plan on bunk beds in a one-bedroom flat over a corner shop.' I wasn't wrong. We arrived at a mansion with lovely gardens, a huge, kidney-shaped swimming pool and enough bedrooms to ensure we occasionally got lost.

One morning I got up early and found our host making coffee in the kitchen. We brought our cups to one of the lounges overlooking the pool. As we gazed at the early sun catching the water he suddenly turned to me and said, 'It's not enough, you know.' I gave him a quizzical look – it was hard to imagine more.

He went on, 'People think that when you have it all, you really *do* have it all. But you don't.' He told me of what he called a 'life-changing experience' that he had just one year before we met. He had become ill and had to have an MRI scan – the procedure that can scan the whole body.

'The consultant showed me my body in the finest detail,' he said. 'I could see my heart, liver, lungs and suddenly it dawned on me that I was human just like everybody else; that I was vulnerable to disease and illness; and, most scary of all, that, like the rest of the world, I too was going to die.

He added, 'I know it sounds stupid, but until that moment I had existed in a make-believe world in which the invulnerability I felt in business would actually protect me against the grim reaper – that somehow I would be able to buy him off, do a deal with him, pay somebody to hide me from him. But on that autumn day in a London hospital, I realised, for the first time in my life, that even if I recovered from my present illness, it was only a respite – one day I was going to die.' He paused and said, 'What I really crave now is not success – I have that. I know it may sound trite, but I want to make a difference.'

My host was involved in a pursuit that will eventually dog all of us. Its roots are deep in every man and woman and if we try to ignore its call then no matter how much money, power or prestige we have, we eventually die inside. It is the search for significance.

If you and I are to discover the heart and soul of success it may be wise not just to consider the 'now', but to try to imagine life some years down the road, take a look back and try to answer the question: *What will matter to me then*? The problem is that when we are young the rules are clear: to get to the top, to have the car parking space marked 'Director', to accumulate sufficient possessions so that people will look and say, 'That is a successful person.' But when we are older it begins to dawn on us that the rules have changed. Now we want not so much to be seen as successful as *significant*. We want to believe that our lives have counted for something – that we have made a difference. We crave not just real estate but relationships. And if that weren't sobering enough, all those we knew in business, who understood the old rules, are suddenly gone. Those who are left will say to us, 'We'll never get by without you.' But they will. The very next day.

The good news is that no matter how old we are, and so long as there is still breath in our body, we can begin the process of change. Alfred Nobel was one of the most successful entrepreneurs of the nineteenth century. In 1867 he patented his new explosive – 'dynamite'. Soon he had patents in every industrialised country. By 1880 he was head of the largest dynamite-producing cartel in the world. Royalties, dividends and profits grew. And then one day a simple mistake changed his life forever. A French newspaper confused the death of Nobel's brother, Ludvig, with his own. Alfred got the opportunity to do what many of us would love to do – he sat down with a cup of coffee, read his own obituary and saw what people had made of his life. But he read phrases like 'merchant of death', and 'his fortune was amassed finding new ways to mutilate and kill'. As Nobel held the newspaper in his hands, he vowed that this was not how he should be remembered, and he decided that, from that very day, his life would be not just successful but significant. He began using his vast wealth to encourage the arts, science and above all peace. Few who watched as Nelson Mandela walked up to the podium in 1995 to collect the Nobel Peace Prize realised that the event was due to the error of a

Swedish journalist who, by his simple mistake, changed another man's life forever.

More and more companies are now getting involved in sharing skills, finance and other resources with communities and charities in need of them. Those of us who watch those companies realise, of course, that they are not just altruistic. When you have employees who strive not just for success but for significance, you have people who cannot help but bring vision into the very companies that are releasing them. I applaud all of this, but, at its heart, the pursuit of significance is achieved individual by individual as those on limited incomes and multimillionaires, office juniors and managing directors, young people and those who are older resolve that whatever our definition of success, it must be larger than a new Jag or the office overlooking the lake.

Giving part of our lives to bringing hope to others brings a sense of perspective. For the past twenty-five years or so we have shared our home with a man who spent most of his childhood years in the care of the local authority. Ron had no home of his own. We invited him to stay for Christmas one night in 1974 and somehow he never left – he's been with us longer than our kids. When he had been with us a short while he got a job as a dustman. That caused some interest among our neighbours. There might have been some homes that had their own cooks and gardeners, but nobody had their own dustman.

Just after Ron came to live with us, I became a partner in the legal practice and they bought me a Mercedes. Without making too many disparaging comments about the car I was driving before that, I can tell you that the jump was immense. I'm sure you can understand that I was just dying to show it off to somebody and I wanted that somebody to be *really* impressed. I chose Ron. As he fastened his seat belt and gazed around in wonder I explained, 'It's called a Mercedes Benz, Ron.' I slipped the car into gear and it glided away. And then – I just couldn't help myself – I put one finger on the steering wheel and moved it around effortlessly. Ron seemed unimpressed. 'It's called "power-assisted steering",' I said.

'Yes, Rob, I know,' he replied. 'We have it on the dustcarts.'

Ron used to be homeless but now he spends some of his spare time working with a soup run in the city centre. One evening I noticed he was wearing old shoes.

'Ron, where are your new shoes?' I asked.

'Oh – I gave them to somebody. I'll save for another pair.'

I'm sure that few would call Ron successful in life, but, in my view, he is. He has worked for over twenty-five years, somehow saved enough to travel the world, including Australia twice, managed a football team, and achieved what many never manage – a little significance.

The problem is that for most of us life is too busy even to consider these issues. But sometimes events conspire to give us time to ponder. Some years ago I was lecturing to a couple of hundred business leaders. I noticed a man at the back of the auditorium who used to come to our seminars regularly but I'd not seen him for a while. In the coffee break I made a beeline for him and told him I'd missed him. He said that two years earlier he had been involved in a serious car accident. He had fought for his life for six months and been on his back recovering for another six. As he spoke I sensed that, against all the odds, some good had come out of this horrendous time. I decided to ask him if my hunch was true.

'Were there any positive elements in this tragedy?'

He answered in a moment: 'Yes – two. First, I had a better appreciation of my wife and children. Before the accident I used to carry their photographs with me to remind me what they looked like. Second, my partners in the office told me I was more use on my back for the last six months of my recovery than I had ever been in the office – because for the first time in twenty-five years at least one of us had *time to think.*'

And that's why, although time management courses can be wonderfully helpful, there's one piece of advice that's normally given that it is absolutely vital to ignore. It's the part that goes something like this: 'Always make the best use of your time. As you drive, listen to motivational tapes. Always have some work in your briefcase to which you can turn if a plane is delayed or a meeting postponed.'

As we come to a close, allow me to share a piece of advice that, by itself, will make this book worth the money you spent. If you are lucky enough to have a few seconds when a phone is not demanding to be answered or a moment when someone is not knocking on your office door asking you to 'spare a minute', then nurture that brief episode. If you're in an airport lounge, don't feel under pressure to get straight on your mobile or to fish some papers out of your briefcase, don't even feel the need to look busy. Instead, buy yourself a coffee, find a quiet corner and enjoy the glorious luxury of *not* making the 'best' use of your time. Just think.

The sheer lack of 'thinking time' – time to smell the roses, to strategise, to let our visions and dreams crystallise, to consider our real priorities – is one of the reasons why many businesses get stuck in a rut. And why, at the start of most time management courses, at least 5 per cent of the delegates ring up to say they are too busy to make it.

And as you sit with your coffee and think, come

back in your mind with me to the business library in which we began and a question asked by a young man of an old 'janitor' – 'What does it mean to be successful – can you make it and still have a life?'

Some years ago a friend of mine, a chartered accountant, was on board a twin-engine plane heading into Chicago Airport. The plane was half owned by his brother-in-law, Rich, and half by the pilot. As they travelled, Matthew was jotting down some life goals. Most of them were material and, he believed, eminently reachable. They concerned the kind of money he would hope to earn in ten years' time, the position he would have in the list of partners on his firm's notepaper and the value of the house he would live in. Rich watched with interest and said, 'Matthew, I need some direction like that – show me how to work out some goals for my life.' Matthew was happy to – he was successful, he was a 'make it happen' man, and, hey, he was getting a free lift anyway.

Just then the pilot turned and said, 'Rich, we have a problem with the port engine.'

Matthew said he felt the atmosphere in the plane

change in a second. They began to lose height. The pilot turned again, this time his voice a little more tense, 'Rich – the red light's come on.'

The words that Matthew heard next seemed to come from another world, another place – certainly not the place that a moment ago had seemed so ordinary, so secure. Rich said, 'Shut the engine down.'

Matthew told me that, in what seemed a millisecond, he looked down at the goals resting on his lap; he then looked out of the left window, saw the propeller stop and turned back to his list. 'These are not my goals!' he whispered under his breath. 'I've got bigger ambitions than these. I want to be a better father, a better husband; I want to leave this world a little better than how I found it.'

By now they had dropped through the cloud and could see the runway. All three knew this was not going to be easy. It's hard to land a two-engine plane on just one, and some pilots never make it. Matthew said, 'As we were coming in, I could see fire engines and ambulances rushing alongside us and then I saw something that looked like a snowplough. The plane hit the runway hard, bucked and skewed, but finally, with my heart practically bursting out of my ribcage, I felt it come to a stop. I turned and gasped out to Rich, "What's the snowplough for?"'

'"Matthew", he replied quietly, "because of our little difficulty they've got jumbo 747's piled up a mile high above us waiting to land and, if we hadn't made it, they just had to get us off that runway fast."'

I don't know for sure whether, if you asked him now, Matthew would tell you he was grateful for that experience, but I sense that he would. He went on to find tremendous success in his career but it never again dominated his life the way it had done previously. It wasn't that he stopped loving his job; it was rather that he saw it in the context of his *whole* life. The carpenter put it like this: 'What does it profit a man to gain the whole world, yet lose his own soul?'

The experience on that July day over twenty years ago changed the future for my friend. What a concept that is – *to change the future*. It was Toffler who coined the phrase. He said, 'It is true that if we do not learn from history we may have to relive it, but if we do not change the future we may have to endure it – and that could be worse.'

It was the small matter of the future that dominated the thoughts of perhaps the most famous businessman of all – Ebenezer Scrooge – in Dickens' *A Christmas Carol*. It would be fair to say that although his business projections seemed to be coming in on the nose, production was up, and cash flow well under control, it had been a dreadful couple of days. He thought he'd got rid of a partner but, as many have discovered since, difficult partners do not disappear so easily.

And Marley's ghost had given Scrooge a vision of what the years ahead held. What he saw horrified him: there are Tiny Tim's crutches resting by the hearth but now with no owner. Scrooge watches as his own belongings are divided up and shared among people who had no respect for him, and finally the ghost takes him to a gravestone, and scrapes the moss away to reveal *his* name. And it is during this traumatic episode that Ebenezer Scrooge, businessman *extraordinaire*, successful in many of the ways that we measure that phenomenon, asks the most incisive question he has ever uttered: 'Are these the shadows of the things that *will* be, or are they shadows of things that *may* be, only? ... Assure me I may yet change these shadows.' In other words, is it too late to change the future?

But is it the case that it requires such a dramatic intervention to make us see more clearly and alter direction a little? Do we all have to pile into small aeroplanes or be whisked by ghosts on a whistle-stop tour of our future in an effort to get our priorities right? Perhaps not, but what is certain is that if anything really matters to us – matters so much that when we are old we want to look back and say, 'This is what I did; this is what I *was*,' – we probably have to begin the process of change: to plant a seed – *today*.

And we probably also have to believe that 120-year-old Jeanne Calment was right: the future is very, very short.

The question asked by the young man of the 'janitor' still hangs in the air: 'Is it possible to make it in business without losing in life?' There may be thousands of young men and women wandering the libraries of our great institutions asking that same question.

But perhaps things are changing. It seems that our business schools at least are waking up to the fact that a *person* in business is a lot more useful than a drone. A Harvard representative said recently, 'We are, of course, as interested as we have always been in ambition and motivation. But we are at the same time just as concerned about the application of those qualities imprudently unchecked by humanity – values, reflection, relationships – *all the things that make one human.*'[19]

When I run seminars I sometimes ask the audience to be still and silent for sixty seconds. People normally indulge me, but after twenty seconds or so I observe that some are distinctly uncomfortable. They begin to shift in their seats, to tap their fingers or gaze around with a worried look on their faces. It took several exercises for the reason for this to dawn on me: these people had not been still for *one minute in the whole of their adult lives*. They had never sat in a quiet room, or walked in a park, or had time for themselves.

Of course I hope you've enjoyed the book but in any event you have done something most people don't do in forty years of working life. You've taken out a few hours to consider 'What is it all for?', 'For whom am I doing it?' and above all '*Why* am I doing it?' Perhaps these questions really are at the heart of success.

And anyway, an old professor would have approved.

NOTES

1   'The Quality of Working Life: 1998 Survey of Managers' Experiences' by the Institute of Management.

2   *Financial Times*, 24 September 1998.

3   *The Times*, 22 January 2000.

4   *The Time Bind* by Arlie Hochschild (Henry Holt & Co., 1997).

5   *Beyond Certainty* by Charles Handy (Hutchinson, 1995).

6   Ibid.

7   *Body and Soul* by Anita Roddick (Ebury Press, 1991).

8   *The Seven Habits of Highly Effective People* by Stephen R. Covey (Simon & Schuster, 1989).

9   *Body and Soul* by Anita Roddick (Ebury Press, 1991).

10   Theodore Roosevelt speaking at the University of Paris, Sorbonne, 23 April 1910.

11   'The Quality of Working Life: 1998 Survey of Managers' Experiences' by the Institute of Management.

12   *Financial Times*, 24 September 1998.

13   *Accountancy Age*, 25 January 2001.

14   *Law Society Gazette*, 11 May 2001.

15 *Law Society Gazette*, 14 June 2001.

16 *Cork on Cork* by Sir Kenneth Cork (Macmillan, 1988).

17 Ibid.

18 *How to Win Friends and Influence People* by Dale Carnegie (Hutchinson, 1990).

19 *New York Times*, 7 December 2000.

letsdolife

I do hope that you've enjoyed *The Heart of Success*. You may want to develop some of the issues a little further either in your company or in your personal life. If so, Letsdolife may be able to help.

Letsdolife can provide a wide range of materials to help you and your employees balance work and home life. One of our newest resources is 'Working to Live', a video-led, stress-awareness training programme. I present the material and the workbook is written by psychologist Dr John Gallacher, one of the UK's leading stress experts.

We run a national programme of *Heart of Success* seminars where I get the chance to explore some of the seven laws in a live setting. We also can provide these seminars on an in-house basis or present some of the materials in a keynote speech – 'The Heart of Success – making a difference in your life and your company'.

We can help your employees find their 'Factor X'

through our advanced Birkman Profiling System. Individuals and teams can be tested and given a comprehensive analysis that will show them how they operate under normal conditions and when under stress, and, perhaps even more importantly, will help them discover what their natural giftings are.

Why not try our 'One Plus One Adventure' weekends, which are designed for a parent and a child between the ages of nine and sixteen? They are in an outdoor adventure setting (with mod cons!) that is just perfect for the parent whose exercise has been limited to walking the office corridors, but which has plenty to challenge the more adventurous. The main aim is to provide parent and child with an unforgettable experience of working, playing and bonding together. Writing in the *Daily Express*, journalist Roland Howard said of his own 'One Plus One' experience with his son, 'Just doing all those things and talking about them has brought us together.'

And, finally, if your company would like to invest some time or money in a little 'dream-catching' – helping a young person fulfil their potential – our team would be pleased to suggest some projects where your involvement would be literally life-changing for a child in challenging circumstances.

A visit to our website will provide details of all our resources – framed copies of the company charter from the 'Believe that the Job You Do Makes a Difference' chapter, research papers and other books, videos and seminar programmes.

It would be good to hear from you.

Rob Parsons

For further information
visit: **www.letsdolife.com**
e-mail: **HOS@letsdolife.com**
telephone: **029 2081 0833**
or fax: **029 2081 1050**